HIS CONSCIOUS PERCEPTION OF THE SOUL

THE EXPLORATION OF WISDOM AND CONTINUOUS INTROSPECTION

ISAIAH A. TISDALE

An Imprint of tbudget, LLC
744 South Street #997
Philadelphia, PA 19147

First tbudget trade paperback edition March 2020

Printed in the United States of America

Library of Congress Control Number: 2020903458
ISBN: 978-1-7346351-0-2 (Paperback)
ISBN: 978-1-7346351-1-9 (eBook)

http://www.isaiahatisdale.com

CONTENTS

INTRODUCTION

"You cannot travel in the path until you have become the Path itself."—Buddha.

In January 2019, the idea to write a book and share my viewpoint sparked. As I was already feeding my mind with spiritual enlightenment, I began to do a lot of research on writing a book.

My reason for writing this book is to inspire others in the way my heightened awareness empowers me to be a better person and live a happy, peaceful life. It is possible to live without conditions. My journey of spirituality allowed me to become closer to my true self. I hope you can use the message in this book as a way to grow closer to your authentic self. I share my perspective and thoughts on consciousness and the soul. I'm using my passage of self-work to not only share but embody an authentic being aligning with wisdom.

My spirit spoke to me and encouraged me to write this book. To be intentional and not focus on good or bad, but to be creative in therapeutic writing. In this book, I want to give a piece of me, providing my thoughts and words as I become closer to my authentic self. I want to allow my creative expression through writing; fill your soul with love and compassion.

My lived experiences and my progressive spiritual journey have made me willing to share my perspective. I have the desire to share my feelings, thoughts, and words to touch individual souls in the universe by promoting awareness and healing. It's my pleasure to share my insights and ideas with the world. I've prevented myself for a long time from being vulnerable and sharing intimate parts of my mind. My restriction has turned to my joy! I'm no longer hostage to conditioning or constraints and open to the evolution of my authentic self!

The idea of self-work is not to recondition but to remove conditions from your life. To be whole as it relates to all aspects of life, especially love and compassion. By helping myself, I'm in a position to help others. To shed light, inspire thought, and spark inquiry internally and externally. I've committed to self-therapy and knowledge expansion through a lens of consciousness. It was essential to spend quality time with myself to rediscover the intimate parts of my mind that I had silenced through conditioning. My trajectory of intuition and higher consciousness is clear. My mind is no longer silent, and I'm open to sharing my powerful words with the universe. My philosophy of leading by example is in the highest order. Let's be one as you join me on this journey of awareness!

There is no better way for me to explain myself than to share content in my journals and real-time reflections. I want to give you a piece of writing that matches the respective messages and deliveries. The overarching message will be evident at the end of the book, but it will have different meanings for different individuals. Content is raw with refined actions of consciousness to express my current state of being. Throughout the book, you'll see many questions I've asked myself as a way to provoke thought and to help your well-being.

Throughout the book, don't be afraid to take notes, ask yourself questions, and reflect. If there is a phrase, sentence, or message that stimulates thought—admit it and free your inner self by further understanding! If you question any word or phrase I mention, you're encouraged to conduct your research to expand your knowledge. As a reader, I like to reflect, seek more understanding if necessary to fulfill my knowledge, and articulate all that has meaning for me. For me, giving responses to questions with profound reasoning was what inspired my mind's expansion. So, throughout the book, I will define terms with my perspective of what they mean to my soul. My mission is to get people to think and listen with an openness of mind and soul!

Why is this book so relevant today? Our ever-changing environment has a desire for the closeness of being. The mental shifts are strides of oneness with yourself and the universe. This book will aid in awareness. In light, my perspective will spark a fire in your soul to consider a life of consciousness. You are the way to soul liberation, so be present in your life to promote awareness.

SECTION ONE

Closing of an unconscious soul

He is me, and I am his perspective.

1

THOUGHTS

"The real mission you have in life is to make yourself happy, and in order to be happy, you have to look at what you believe, the way you judge yourself, the way you victimize yourself."—Don Miguel Ruiz.

Reaching the soul is like digging for treasure that's present, but why does it seem so difficult to achieve? We must first unclutter the baggage we've been holding for years and unpack our underlying emotions and reasoning. Then challenge any existing perceptions that exist in our lives to free our minds from domestication and unveil new thoughts.

But how can you introduce new thoughts when your current beliefs consume you? Ask yourself:

- Are you always in deep thought?
- Are you lost in your world?
- Are you thinking all the time about everything?

- Do you feel mentally trapped by your thinking?
- Do you believe you are unable to shut off your thinking?

I'm here to tell you it's possible to stop thinking when you want and embrace the present moment.

Now ask yourself, are you where you want to be in life? I'll affirm you're where you ought to be in life. Life will take some unexpected turns but, for the greater good. Through reflection, we'll realize that we are much further than we expected in our lives at the moment and that everything has happened for a reason. If this revelation doesn't seem familiar, sit back, and think of how you've overcome events in life, and how you became the best version of yourself. We are all designed for success, and fear is powerless with awareness.

All egos root in fear. What does the ego mean? The state of unconsciousness of thoughts, words, or actions. The past overflows the ego with conditions in life. In the future and past, the ego prospers as its inability to live in the present moment requiring consciousness. It's structured to keep us unconscious in a state of suffering. This suffering ends at this moment. To free ourselves of ego, we must avoid internalizing, personalizing, and unpacking our feelings. We must recognize and understand a sense of discomfort that can transcribe in shadow work. The short-term impact of the reaction does not overpower the liberation of consciousness of the soul.

Fear fortifies our ignorance. We tend not to welcome wisdom that battles our existing beliefs and not back the ego. This fear transpires into ignorance about self and unconsciousness.

How to rediscover our consciousness? Acknowledge your inner being that exists with the ability to connect to our higher level of power or Divine. There is an understanding that a central universe is present in every being where we interconnect. Many layers of consciousness drive the world. Our awareness brings forth a state unparalleled to the ego. What does this require? Authenticity.

What is authentic? Truth and acceptance. It's the pure state of everything. So, what is a genuine being? It's the actual state of being with the alignment of the soul and intent of our higher power. So, what is a higher power? You! The ability you have to shed light on the universe channeling the great Divine! To emerge to our authentic being, we must accept:

- Conditioned thinking is the unconscious accumulation of ideas. The ideas come from the traumas or beliefs of other people.
- Domestication is intentional or unintentional actions created by a person or group of people to be a certain way.

Emerge

But can we save ourselves in fear? What does that look like? Fear is an illusion created by the ego. Naturally, we are fearless beings that were condition to experience fear. Fear has many forms. We save ourselves from fear by reshaping the way we think and escaping negative thought patterns that will keep fear alive. For example, worry describes repeated negative thought patterns disregarding the moment. The unintentional addiction to negativity arises through the focus of the past or future. The ego manifests in fearful thinking by multiplying negative emotions to combat your spirit.

The idea of spirit will conflict with the ego. One of our greatest philosophers, Plato, reasoned that spirit is the noble white horse on the right. The mind is unfavorable to injustice, and the spirit is favorable to face and overcome challenges. It is victorious with honor through adversity. Our judgment can never cloud the reason that forces us to think, analyze, look forward, and incorporate perspectives to decide what is best. There is an application of reason in our awareness movement, together with an intuition of trust and knowledge in our every decision.

Intuition is our soul speaking to our presence in the universe. It is the calling of a higher power. Intuition is powerful and real, and you must refrain from allowing the ego's inauthentic nature to consume your natural intuition.

There is a straightforward word to consider in the face of the ego: self. The depths of its meaning is beyond the selfish context created in our world. It exists in the realm of centeredness and the connection to your authentic self. This is the temple of pure unconditional love and the place where our actual therapy takes place. We should remind ourselves of these ideals and not resort to conditioned thinking of the word, self, but give back it's true meaning! The intention to restore the meaning requires us to destroy the external noise and be authentic.

Why do we allow disturbance to impact our consciousness? How can awareness increase in moments of disturbance? The disruption I'm talking about is our lack of support for the present moment, and the disorder I'm talking about is our lack of support for the present moment.

Our resistance to presence keeps us locked into the past or future. We must surrender to the moment without resistance. We often refuse to understand surrendering as long as our opposition to wisdom exists. The ego powers this resistance to keep us disconnected from our authentic self.

Why is the state of "being" so difficult? The idea of letting go can be challenging for many people. Surrendering to the present moment and facing reality will uncover the ego that concealed our true self. There is a huge fear we face in our society for one to be with their true self. It's easier to build falsified images of yourself than to honor our authentic being.

Grow

Fear is a signal for growth—the call for growth towards more love, which has a holistic application to life. Love can be a reference to any and everything in life. The best challenger for fear is love—unconditional love. There is no reason to hold on to fear when love is always available in our spirit. The signal for growth gives us a way to identify areas where we can evolve as an authentic being. To acknowledge fear without identifying with it or consuming it calls for a reality check.

Do you feel like you can't live without fear? Has fear becomes part of your daily life, holding you back from your full potential? We have self-created fear of conditioning and old thought, which is different from our nature to avoid danger or threats. As we grow older, the conditioned thinking we acquired, creates a separate mind and self that removes us from our authentic self.

Think about this: After hurt, do you become a more loving and compassionate person? Or do you create resentment and revenge? The first question reveals a way forward as a representation of the realization to appreciate life's lessons. The second question suggests that you may be in the past without considering moving forward and expressing negative energy. Why can't we love without getting wrapped up in suffering? We have a condition to suffer when we experience loss or pain. Is it possible to shift that frame of mind through higher awareness? Do we unintentionally create our misery?

Your constant battle with your ego exists because of the superiority and inferiority complex of your false self and other beings. The ego survives by our unconscious surrendering of power, and it creates a complex of inequality with other people. There is a seesaw effect with ego and our thoughts. There are moments where the ego will inject ideas of being better or worse than another individual, and that lifts or drops our feelings at the same moment. Awareness is the key to overcome this battle so that you can no longer see yourself as being unequal in the universe. We are all equal beings and have a real voice in the world.

Entitlement is one of the many voices of the ego, the belief that someone is more deserving and has a higher right to something. There is a projection of this attitude onto others, and this also causes a sense of fear within entitlement placed by conditions. This type of fear has two horns: thoughts of scarcity and insignificance in life.

Often people lack the mentality of abundance in the universe, revealing a state of mind that only sees shortage. The mindset of scarcity can come from abuse or wrongdoing throughout life. This entitled behavior creates superior beliefs that you deserve more than the rest of the people because of your past and present circumstances. This view can create the need to get all that you can from anyone to fill the gap with limited thoughts, and not see any issue with the practiced behavior.

On the other horn, lack of self-value in the universe

affirms the fear of insignificance in life. The trait all entitled individuals have is the manipulation to fulfill their desires. Entitlement comes with pushing personal responsibility to other people to fill a void. This responsibility is unfair and disregards compassion for other people. You ought to be able to identify this voice of the ego and set boundaries to silence any sense of entitlement in your world.

Make this promise to yourself:

I will not allow other people's sense of entitlement command control in my life. I will protect my sense of awareness and peace.

Look at yourself, what do you see in the mirror? Is this image conditional (i.e., clouded by external factors)? Do you feel free from self-suffering? Does self-doubt exist in this mirrored image? How can you be your best self? Now, take this moment to regain your power, freeing yourself from thought by accepting the picture, and realizing that the impermanence of being is the only truth. Now be willing to embrace life and fill your spirit with wisdom that promotes love.

There is a condition to internalize our experiences from our surroundings that helped shape our false self-image. Don't give your negative words, life, and don't give your negative thoughts, power.

These observations can impact our concepts of success and failure. Everyone has a personal definition of what forms a success or failure, which is subjective. We must not get caught up in other's interpretations, but to define our success and flip our identified shortcomings into learning experiences. To be your best self in any situation, trust yourself and your capabilities. We have the power to self-conceptualize.

I would like to zoom in on learning; our state of mind impacts our ability to learn. If we're not willing to learn, the brain will not absorb any valuable content. If we're ready, things will seem much more precise and applicable in our lives. We should always be receptive to new learning experiences as this will aid in our evolution of beings.

Ask yourself: are you growing to survive, or are you growing to live? This question brings forth our honesty in reality and awakens the desire for a shift in our life.

What is desire? An intuitive expression of our inner being aspiration. Often, our desires get clouded by the ego. So, we must be sure to question if our ambitions are true to our authentic self. Our desires can shift, but it should always be genuine. Any deceptive desires implanted from ego are inauthentic to our being.

Are you conscious of your desires and intentions? The purity and trueness of both concepts that come from the soul. Closure, as it relates to any aspect of life, is not needed for your growth, but sometimes, the ego can hide in your crave for closure to prevent your highest self from expression. Are you hiding behind excuses to remain stagnant in your life? Or are you ready to accept the call for action to foster growth?

Accept

When your intentions and intuition are clear, it is pure intent without the ego. What is intention? This is the use of authentic power, which includes beingness of presence. Intuition is our natural consciousness. The thought we get when something seems wrong. Intuition is a combination of our authentic emotions and feelings.

Be conscious of what story you're telling about your reality. Reality is your personal experience-this experience created through your perception. What questions are you always asking yourself? Or is your mind always creating your impression? The mind can control your beingness through conditioning and unawareness. Observe any thoughts or words you're attached to and given permanence in your life; that's an illusion of power created. Always be honest and stand in your truth without painting a story through the ego.

The ego creates the feeling that something is not real, and your soul knows it's true. Your ego is not your true self —it is your unconscious self, masked as "who you are." Our intuition is the voice of our soul, which speaks to us in life situations. Your soul is who you are.

Do you allow your limiting beliefs to influence other's behavior intentionally? What does this say about your state of mind? With fears, are you holding back from your limitless being? Find the answers within yourself and unmuzzle the voice of your soul. All thoughts are not true to your authentic nature as your unconsciousness may be present. We don't judge these thoughts, but we should be able to identify when these thoughts of unawareness run through our minds.

We sometimes give racing thoughts power over the mind. This power shows up in our inability to be clear and aware of thoughtful expression. These racing thoughts can become hurtful when we allow the ego to get involved and voice malice for its satisfaction. Racing thoughts may appear in free-thinking to examine circumstances, but once ego joins this cycle, it becomes anguished thinking.

Why fixate on something you cannot change? The fixation may include a person of interest, a position in time, the past or the future. My observation is that people tend to try to shift things they struggle internally with and become fixed on the external form of their issue. I would like to zone in on a person of interest. The obsession form as deception, drawing you to this person because you can relate to them but, feeds the ego. The fixation on the person of interest is to help you identify your internal issues.

The challenge is acknowledging your concerns and understanding that you are in an unconscious state of mind. But the struggle is the removal of something—we need to be comfortable letting go of bad habits for our higher conscious being. The reality is that both parties need to be in a position to help themselves separately, instead of feeding the ego. You cannot do the work for someone else, and someone else cannot do the work for you. This action provokes fear in our false being by attempting to get to know our true self and encouraging development in someone else. There is the potential of outgrowing our false existence. These fearful actions hinder our evolution, holding on to a moment that passes inevitably.

There is a contradiction to attempt to shift someone's state of being when you're unwilling to commit to shifts in your life. How can we try to enforce an action when we're not exemplifying that action? We must observe our thoughts, words, and acts first before introducing something that doesn't exist in our own life.

How can you help someone when you're not happy with yourself? We must be honest and real with ourselves. We can only help someone else when we have provided resolution in our own life.

We sometimes recognize the unhealthiness of someone's behavior, but still, allow our unconscious self to react in the same way. For example, our present society consumes social media and the creation of a social image. Often, this follows a falsified portrayal of authentic character that either fits in or stands out. False social personas recognized and valued at the same time. People try to find a social status to confirm their existence and live two separate lives (one on social media and one in reality) or one false reality. There are negative thoughts manifested by the ego to avoid looking into your authentic self. Living a life of authenticity is more comfortable than a fabricated life full of unstoppable negative thoughts.

We can acknowledge that in situations, your false self is feeling the negative emotions, not your authentic self, because your authentic self only recognizes negative emotions, and do not manifest. Your false self often manifests negative emotions to stroke your ego and deepen your unconsciousness. Your false self is self-serving, not all-serving.

When you continuously ask: why me? You become a victim of situations. You've isolated yourself as the only being who is facing hardship without considering that others are going through issues as well, so you're not alone. The reality is for a cause, you're going through this situation, and it intends for you to learn from the situation. Don't miss up on the opportunity to grow and stop being a victim of circumstances. Instead of asking why me, begin by asking what the lesson is in the situation. Don't play victim to a situation as it leads to missing the message and clouds resolution. So, embrace the situation without identifying with it, understand the purpose, and be free to infinite potential.

Do you feel you're enough? Do you accept you're capable of anything, including love? Do you feel full of endless possibilities? Our setbacks come from our unrealized potential. We don't see how remarkable we are and the power we bring to the universe. It is of a high order to regain this power and expel any ideas of not feeling enough. There is a fear of presence when not feeling enough, and this fear comes from our distorted reality and preconceived feelings from conditioning.

Do you believe your words shape your reality? The way you use words can impact your life in either an uplifting or depressing way. Words produce thought; thought becomes a reality. We often disregard the power of words and the influence over our existence. For example, negative self-talk can break your spirit and able to cloud the truth in the light. We often see how this type of talk can take someone to the edge and dark places to escape their reality. Our awareness in the use of words is essential to our constructed reality.

In reality, layers of pain will build up if you continue to avoid the current issues taking authority. Avoidance will create self-suffering or self-inflicting pain. We have choices when it comes to the pain; we either leave the pain inside or get rid of the pain through healing.

We fragment reality and think by compartmentalizing situations and events, instead of looking at the big picture as a whole. This fragmented reality was a personal habit of mine. I noticed excuses made through segmentation are not healthy for growth. How can we rid ourselves of these mental illusions we create? By being more present.

What is that one thing holding you back? For me, it was vulnerability. This underutilized power and became strong beyond imagination. Try to think about one thing that has been closing off your next evolutionary stage.

Evolve

The essence of obedience to your fulfillment requires to set the thought of who you want to be and be flexible to the ever-changing nature of being. There are times when things may not always align, but you've to recognize Divine timing and continue to be intentional.

Thought visualization is using your mind and the power of intention to create your reality. Thoughts you embed in your mind come through your existence. Your thoughts link to the things you do in life. We have control over our thoughts. We choose to give power to the ego by releasing our energy to it. Use your ability to build your life inwardly and capture images created by your true self to live a conscious life by self-intention. The use of thought visualization empowers positive thinking. There is positive energy expressed through visualization, aligning your authentic being with reality. There is comfort in writing your thoughts down that helps visualize perception. While reading your words, help you understand your level of consciousness.

Why does consciousness matter in our universe? Because of compassion, happiness, and love matters. Our awareness of ourselves, others, and the world have a positive impact on us—the reflection of your need for consciousness in the universe. A piece of mind can create real prosperity in your life. There should be discernment in the choices we make as we should always use our acquired wisdom when making a decision. The idea of regret should never exist as we use insight to eradicate any self-disappointment. We should consider accountability and responsibility for our choices.

Consciousness impacts unconditional love. What does love mean to you? The choice to be utterly vulnerable by granting access to your being without conditions. What is your full nature? The combination of physical, emotional, mental, and spiritual being. To love others all around and accept them without conditions.

The idea of love being a choice goes along with our intention, and our determination should be to love without conditions. I've defined love through my perception and life experiences. Our definitions of love depend on our personal view of the concept. There are consistencies with the description of love: acceptance and understanding. Our definition of love often disregards the root of its make-up: self-love. Frequently, this concept is overlooked because the expression of love is primarily external in society, as internal love is not always at the center. But how can you love unconditionally without loving yourself unconditionally? The feelings of unconditional love without unconditional self-love becomes ego-centered. Your conditions take control through attachment, fear, and unrealized self-value.

We create intentional and unintentional barriers to love. These barriers form protection from vulnerability, hurt, and access to our full potential as beings of love. Identify environments where you can enhance love. These are free flow areas for love that will allow you to invoke loving thoughts. The real road to happiness is for you to love yourself and all of humanity. Happiness should be unconditional, as true love is unconditional. Happiness derives from love, and one cannot exist without the other. External love is not at the extent of self-love. There should never be a sacrifice of one to choose the other; there should be universal, unconditional love.

Observe your thoughts through consciousness; don't judge your egoic thoughts. Your perspective can be multidimensional if you're channeling your consciousness. As a being of many dimensions, you don't have one element, as the multitude of your awareness can create different understandings. For example, we can see through the view of unconsciousness at the same time as we see through the lenses of consciousness and construct conclusions. Our conclusions build on many factors from our presence. Do yourself service and explore these dimensions by observation. Genuinely get to know yourself, and all you have to offer the universe. Our many aspects are fortification of our authentic power.

When are you going to begin healing your thoughts? The transformation of your mental capacity to expand your awareness is a need in the process. Relinquish attachment to your thoughts because we are not our thoughts, but we should be conscious of our thoughts. This healing is gradual and requires commitment. So, I ask, are you ready to give up disoriented thoughts to move into greatness?

Move

The acceptance of reality and responsibility for our reactions is essential to our presence in the universe. When we accept the fact, we can create our reality through consciousness. Enlightenment will shape our reality by shifting our minds and way of thinking. We have control over our emotions and thoughts. It takes awareness to harvest this control:

- Allow your Divine nature to transform your thoughts.
- Fill your mind of thoughts that serve your consciousness.
- Encourage progressive thinking to alter your creative reality.

- No longer hold on to limiting beliefs that go against your higher self.

You remain disconnected from the source of the Divine due to personal fears created by the ego. Do you find it challenging to grasp the idea of impermanence?

What is impermanence? This is the plan that all things must end, and nothing is forever. Even suffering comes to an end if we allow for enlightenment. How does this play in your fear of things ending? We all understand things come to an end, but we don't want to face the fact. When something ends, it hit on a personal level; we harvest this fear to comfort our ego.

I'll share some thoughts I have to live by and balance every day. Such thoughts include: put me first; be resilient; be mindful; don't take things personally; the world is more important than me; be happy and be thankful for existence. These daily reminders humble my spiritual presence in the universe.

The ego is impatient, which prompted my foster for patience in my life. I struggled with patience because I wanted things done when I felt they should. This desire has control by the ego to possess power over outcomes. The impatient nature of my being that existed altered my reality. I was a real-life example of the attitude: why wait? I was never irrational as I always thought about the things that stood in my decisions, but I didn't practice patience. This unwillingness to allow things to run its course often ended in disappointment. My thoughts were always going a million miles per minute and, at times, taking me away from the present moment. My intentional practice of patience has made me more assured of my self-work and presence.

I know you're asking yourself how long the self-work

will take to see a shift in your reality? There is no defined answer:

- Be willing to surrender your false self.
- Be introduced to your authentic self.
- Be patient and understand self-work is forever.
- Be aware of the moment of now and apply consciousness.

Acceptance of these things removes time from the equation and focuses on self-guidance as a more conscious being in the universe. Allow your soul to inform your mind of what your authentic nature needs to hear to be more present.

Reflect

1. What does your authentic self mean to you? What does living an authentic life mean to you?
2. Fear. What do you fear? Why do you fear that thing(s)? How does it make you feel?
3. Love. What do you love? Why do you love that thing(s)? How does it make you feel?
4. List things that you would like to remove from your life
5. List things that you would like to include in your life

2

LISTEN

"Silence is the great teacher and to learn its lessons you must pay attention to it. There is no substitute for the creative inspiration, knowledge, and stability that come from knowing how to contact your core of inner silence."— Deepak Chopra.

"In human intercourse, the tragedy begins, not when there is misunderstanding about words, but when silence is not understood."—Henry D. Thoreau.

We're encouraged to talk more instead of listening and feel like we can fix people and the universe instead of understanding. We learn to speak better, but there is not enough practice on how to listen better. There are constant reminders to hear, but there is no context for how to listen and how to be attentive when someone speaks. This dilemma is widespread in the universe. How can we move past the conditioned behavior to be avid speakers and not listeners? How can we balance both in our life? First of all, we must remove our conditioning and be open to a life of balance that will advance our authentic being. We allow our conditioning to take over our lives, unknowingly. The implications are never clear until awareness awakens in our lives.

There is a quality of listening in life:

- Listening to intuition.
- Listening to other beings.
- Listening to the messages of the universe.

When you're always talking more than you listen, you're not paying attention to the message. You'll find yourself waiting for a turn to speak and often interrupt others while they are talking. Your efforts to control and dominate a conversation is evident. But it may not be the control you seek; it can be your way of expression and release of thoughts. Have you ever considered surrendering to the present moment and understanding ideas? You learn so much by just listening and watching body language. It's okay to take some time to think about a response after someone finishes speaking. It shows that you were more focused on listening than on having a reply readily available for rebuttal.

The most important thing is practicing the skill of attentive listening. Make the goal to listen without judgment.

Judge

Our ego will find faults in any position to prevent us from listening attentively and personalizing our defense position. We need to be more conscious in any form of communication. Don't jump to conclusions, listen. Be sure to consider another's point of view. Our conditioned mind tends to jump to conclusions without full information based on our perspective. The purpose of listening is not to share your point of view or to jump to any conclusions, but to consider the point of view of others without sharing your own, unless requested. Does this include complaining?

Complaining has purpose and intent attached. We must be aware of the result we're trying to drive and reason for action. First, think about the positive things in a situation (most things are not completely bad). Focus on the experience you're gaining and the things you're learning. Secondly, do not subdue yourself to endless complaints. Find the real value in the present and allow it to manifest itself in a positive way to break any conditional thinking of complaining as normal. Listen to yourself as you complain! Bring awareness to the moment.

When asking someone to fulfill a request, we need to be mindful after receiving a response. Sometimes we take the answers personal due to the person's inability to fulfill our request. So, we must ask ourselves, does that request transform into a demand? That results in one safe answer without criticism. We must listen to ourselves when making a request and also listen to the other person's response. We should either not take them personally as we understand requests are binary: yes or no. The ego may be present when you feel the need to ask why your request cannot be fulfilled, as a specific response that you may have expected and not received. Be able to listen and observe when this moment is happening.

How do you feel when someone is not listening when you're asking a question, advice, or insight? Being fully aware of my feelings when someone is not listening, I always make a conscious effort for any conversation to be present. Also, I'm learning to ask permission to share if necessary, which allows the other person to be more receptive to any shared information. It's important to let someone request your feedback, which gives that person the ability to listen and appreciate your share of feedback from a place of sincerity. Refrain from unsolicited advice and opinion. If you're not asked, don't feel entitled to share because it's not about you at this moment. We don't always have to share when it's not needed, just listen, be present, and add more value if requested.

Be mindful of the content you put on the universe. The things you say are materials in the world. There are repercussions for anything wrongly said, so be sure to take accountability. It becomes impossible to judge when you listen and understand. The root causes create empathy. Understand the emotional context and the purpose of conversations. Make it your intention to become a better listener. You've to make an effort to shift your attention, then make sure care is present when listening to someone's idea instead of passing judgment.

Superficial communication has created a significant impact on our society. We are dwelling in surface-level connections and discussions. People love to get caught up in any story to escape their reality. We see this in gossip, testimonies, and venting by another person. We are avoiding any depth of conversation as we may not know how to explore further because of our reluctance to create depth within ourselves. We must be more aware of superficial habits as it pertains to discussions. We need to listen to our inner being in every encounter and moment. We should refrain from contradicting our authentic desires—the need for closeness to someone root in the exploration of different experiences and open conversations.

Open

Be able to receive the provided information. Make the experience a valuable exchange. Only share what you can share, and if you have not processed an internal piece of information, be careful before sharing to avoid creating resentment from sharing.

Self-check yourself: are you talking more than you're listening? Are you thinking more than you're listening? Ask yourself these questions in active listening as a way to keep yourself in line and give your full attention to the effort. Altruism comes in hand with the practice of listening. This selflessness concerns the well-being of others and allows us to be compassionate to anyone. The willingness to help can appear when someone is speaking, taking time to listen, be generous with our presence and time. There is a sense of joy in altruistic behavior as it relates to our moral inclination as spiritual beings.

The ability to listen attentively is essential not only for our well-being but also for building relationships. To be able to pay close attention to the matter is a gift as you refrain from exercising selective listening and giving your time. For example, our elders have abundant wisdom to share, but our ego prevents the absorption of their lived experiences. We refrain from setting aside time to explore their mind and share our presence. Imagine how your relationship with your grandparents would or would be if you set aside time to engage and listen to what they have to say. I'm talking about deep conversations that make the ego uncomfortable because of awareness efforts to get all the things you would like to know to have complete information or get a different perspective.

The separation of two people in open dialogue resides in

the ability to listen. Are you paying attention to your authentic self, or are you too disconnected? How is your intuition playing a role? Listen to the message presented in front of you. Refrain from escaping what is in plain sight and welcome realness through listening. The ego plays a massive part in neglecting intuition and power to listen.

Check your intentions! Are you waiting for a rebuttal? Are you looking for a time to say what you always wanted to say—now have the opportunity? Are you looking to manipulate the conversation? Do you plan to make this moment about you? Do you genuinely want to listen, understand, and support in any way possible (if granted permission)?

Are you compassionate while listening? Allow the moment for an individual to explore their thoughts without interruption while using silence as a way to open another person's mind freely. When you're listening, are you comprehending everything? Are you open to the content and processing accordingly? Have you ever considered your volume of voice while you're speaking, and how it plays into the openness of others to share? It's challenging to practice listening when you're always trying to overpower the conversation with the volume of your voice. Most people become less reluctant to take part in discussions when they feel that others are overwhelming. Allow someone else to drive the conversation and be aware of your compulsion to speak.

Are you willing to shift through the capacity of listening? Be able to respond to your inner voice through the shifting effort and focus of your life. How can we promote holistic listening in our lives? Does this encompass internal and external listening?

Focus

How present are you at this moment? Have you ever paid attention to your breathing while listening? If you never, start now. This practice brings forth presence. Our breath has a way of leveling our inner being and maintaining calmness. Breathing helps send away any anxious or uncomfortable feelings of the body and mind. You can be in a place and not be present. It's like being in a home and still not present. What prevents us from being present? The ego.

Repeat this:

I surrender to the reality of things and the present moment.

Offer your presence when you read and write. When reading words, please stop and understand the message expressed. By reading, allow moments of reflection and listen to the authentic message that resonates with your being. When writing, listen to your genuine thoughts, and be honest. Do not allow the ego to take over spreading unawareness and dishonesty to your nature. Through writing, there is self-accountability and mental clarity. Listen to yourself; be present.

How can you share your knowledge with others? To be open to listening to issues attentively and sharing valuable responses when appropriate. Send encouraging words, ask insightful questions, and share your unique perspective. It's essential to thrive in environments with promoted knowledge sharing.

In the moment of sharing, step into the person's mind and observe what is being disclosed and revealed emotionally. When a person speaks, emotions are always present, whether intentional or unintentional. At the moment, show empathy without getting caught up in the story. Focus on your observation and content provided by the person to give full attention. Be appreciative of the shared information from the person; maintain a level of interest when listening and be attentive. Disengagement reduces your willingness to listen, following your effectiveness of hearing. Be sure to give the attention you would desire when someone talks. Do on to others what you want to be done to you.

Our mobile devices affect our ability to be present. Mobile devices can distract you from listening and being present in a conversation. They divide our attention and alter our focus. Try to refrain from using mobile devices during conversations. Be aware of any distractions when someone is speaking. Eye contact is essential. Avoid texting, scrolling social media, or watching television when someone is sharing.

Our sobriety impacts our ability to be present. Being sober is to be present, as not being sober clouds your ability to be present at the moment—it puts you in a state without presence. This sedated state disables alertness and sound judgment while creating difficulty in listening to shared information.

What are your thoughts while someone is speaking? Are your thoughts someplace else or at the moment? Is it about yourself or the other person? Are you waiting for a chance to speak or willing to listen? Share your presence by listening and give gratitude for the moment of connection. Hearing costs nothing but open ears and a state of presence. Stop, listen, and embrace the moment (i.e., self, people, and environment).

Learn

Instead of allowing external situations to force reactions, go inside and ask yourself why a particular instance trigger your emotions? Why are you letting so many emotions to release in this situation? Most likely, your reactions have nothing to do with the situation and everything to do with your internal frame of mind. These are moments of awareness if you're attentive and willing to listen.

The ego has a way of preventing us from understanding to keep us in a state of unawareness. Voice out when you're not understanding or need clarity, so you won't get lost and be able to follow the context. This time for clarity is significant because it can create a higher flow of engagement while keeping your attention. Never get to a point and be like "I'm lost," find a way back to an understanding before you accept defeat. Don't give power to misunderstanding as you have a nature of intelligence.

We must go to the root of listening: self. Why do you find it difficult to listen? Why do you refuse to listen to yourself (i.e., feelings, intuition, and thoughts)? How has your upbringing affected your ability to be attentive (i.e., family dynamics and social environment)? Do your settings allow you to listen and increase understanding? What can you do now to make you more conscious to listen when someone is speaking (i.e., take accountability and be the change in your life, now)?

Why do we struggle with conversations? Why are tough conversations, not practice at home or in school? Can we move past this by practicing today and any day forward? We must let go of fear!

Our current state of listening goes back to our conditioning of listening. Listening as a child:

- Were you open to what others had to say?

- Did you disregard anything anyone had to say?
- Did you listen with love and compassion?
- Did you just listen enough for a response (i.e., not attentively but to serve the ego)?

Being heard as a child:

- What did the expression of your thoughts look like?
- Were you only heard in certain circumstances or always heard?
- After your parents hear you out, was there a retaliation? Or was love and compassion nurtured?

Listening to ourselves:

- How was your intuition fostered (i.e., trusting the intuitive nature of the soul without egoic influence)?
- Were you allowed to listen and think freely?
- How was listening practiced in your household?
- Did your parents or guardians listen to what you had to say? Or where you continuously silenced or overpowered by their voice (i.e., making it challenging to hear yourself)?

The reflection on these questions may help identify the conditioning of listening in your life. The power of acknowledgment and acceptance leads us to the truth of our false reality. Listening strengthens intimacy with oneself and others, so setting our foundation can impact our ability to be present now.

We can discourage our curiosity; I wasn't comfortable asking questions, and I held on to the fear of asking questions. By asking questions, our awareness intensifies as we are becoming more knowledgeable. We should never allow fear to hold us back from our curiosity. I've learned the power of asking questions as I was one who refrained from asking questions. Instead, I used my abilities of cleverness and resourcefulness to answer my questions. I've learned that there is more completeness in information and efficiency in asking questions. By asking questions, you gain a further understanding of the task or topic. I understood it was adequate to ask myself questions for new knowledge. But, it was not enough to depress my questions on understanding with others. I no longer allow not to ask questions in the way to reach my full potential; instead, I make sure I asked questions to ensure clarity. This practice helps me not only in my personal and professional life but on my spiritual journey. By asking questions, I'm able to reach depth within myself to make things more transparent.

Ask questions if you're unsure. These questions can be internal or external. You can ask questions directly (to the person) or indirectly (to yourself). Pinpoint something you would like to understand further as a way to be present.

Take every experience as a learning experience and focus on the message. Take that message and further use it with greater understanding and commitment. Continue to ask questions every second, every minute, and every day. This habit leads to uncovering lessons.

Be sure to draw out the lessons in any situation. Lessons provide a new perspective on situations. Also, lessons consider purpose in the reasoning of conditions. Often, we overlook that valuable information and negative parts of a situation are the focus. The realization of lessons usually kicks in long after. What if we could reflect on experiences earlier on and refrain from focusing on the negative aspects? This process is part of positive reframing that encourages comprehension of purpose. This idea of purpose always seems complicated at moments when our mind is not the clearest. We have incredible brain capabilities that help us process information quickly. Let's put that power to use in situations and divert from negativity by taking notice of Divine lessons.

Be open to listening to your inner voice. Personal listening is synonymous with the art of listening externally. Don't shut your inner voice down, instead embrace it through attentiveness. Be tuned in to the frequency of receiving through listening. Your higher self answers the reception. The only thing you need to give is presence. It becomes easy to recognize your wholeness in being through listening. We are all whole beings, and recognition takes awareness. Be gentle with yourself while listening and be aware of the energy that you are displaying. Show your presence at the moment.

Be able to listen to your internal suffering and have the willpower to release it from your soul. The answers are in front of you when you listen. So, can connection and intimacy with your inner self build by listening? If we choose to commit to this creation of exchange, there can be a more in-depth understanding of listening.

Emerge

There is so much therapy in allowing someone to talk and just listen. I'm talking about healing in both ways. For the other person, as they get things off their mind, hopefully, process feelings and thoughts to come to informed resolutions. For you, as you create an understanding of an individual, give comfort, reflect, and provide advice if asked. This insight enforces care, compassion, and empathy.

By speaking less, your perspective becomes more valuable when another person solicits it. Your view becomes more powerful as you can listen attentively to content while observing feelings and thoughts. You're no longer waiting to reply but, listening to respond if needed.

You get a deeper understanding of humanity by listening. Social issues become more evident. Agreement or disagreement moved to the back burner, and presence remains at the forefront. There is a need for open ears to serve humanity. There is a call of action declared through clarity of issues.

Just listen! Listen to your natural connection to the universe. The universe speaks to us through the interconnectedness that exists in energy. The energy exerted through frequencies and vibrations signal responses. Being able to pay attention to the energy transmitted from the universe enhance our state of awareness.

Transformative listening includes all six senses (i.e., sight, hearing, smell, taste, touch, and intuition). The feeling of intuition plays a significant part in transformative listening. In reality, there is self-realization through our sense of intuition. There are emerging opportunities for self-development and projection of intuition to help others.

Listening and application go together as they are both ways to improve our life. To apply, you must first be willing to listen. Be sure to give everyone the same attention given and respect their openness to share. Treat others as your equal, and the other person becomes the focus of transformative listening. Use a state of reflection after transformative listening.

The power in transformative listening is awareness and presence. Through awareness, the purpose, concerns, or need are easily identifiable. Through presence, you give the other person your full self without the ego.

You champion for others while they speak through the availability of care and compassion. This action adds value to both ends, self, and others. Transformative listening occurs on multi-levels: self, other people, and the world. Deep connection truly blooms! There is a sense of joy in transformative listening as the expression of your authentic self is in action.

Are you listening to healing opportunities inwardly? Your identified areas of healing. Are you strengthening your inner being? Be sure to listen to any internal disturbances that arise mentally, emotionally, physically, and spiritually. Be the advocate for your healing process. As an advocate, you will only succeed by taking notice of the inner being. There is healing in listening. Be conscious of your inner emotions when listening.

You already have all the answers inwardly, even though we use external experiences to respond to how we process things in our lives. No one can tell you something you already know but haven't uncovered. Seek internally and dig deep, but always listen to your inner voice. Magnify your inner voice while doing self-work to establish higher consciousness.

Excellent internal communication is essential to external communication. We miss messages from the Divine by not listening—cues giving to us to reduce suffering and make life easier. The ego tends to divert us from listening to end suffering. I'm not following the voice of the deceiver.

Listening is a spiritual discipline. There is not enough

emphasis on this discipline. For instance, meditation, prayer, and yoga all require listening, listening to your inner voice, your center of being, and your breath. We must learn the art of listening without condition and use our ability to be more aware of the universe.

We are always giving warnings, but we must use our discernment to listen. Refrain from ignoring your intuition and follow the sound of the soul. We find unconditional love by listening to our inner being. Be attentive to the responses of the soul and choose to be present with your-self. This attention opens a dimension that emerges authentic love.

Reflect

1. By listening to your authentic being, write down three lessons you learned in the past year.
2. By listening to your authentic being, write down changes of self in the past two years.
3. Allow your inner voice to speak, listen, and answer: how do you handle a bad day or conflict?
4. Today, share any words of wisdom to the universe.
5. How true are you to your authentic self when listening? How does your ability to listen empower your higher self attentively?

3

FEELINGS

"If what you are thinking doesn't make you feel good, change that thought. Bad cannot bother you unless you are available."—Iyanla Vanzant.

It's easy to become comfortable with a state of unhappiness. Especially through continuous "disappointment," "unfavorable circumstances," and "insecurities." We have all developed definitions of what these unhappy states mean to us and the implications for our personal life. We've unconsciously created these states continuing our suffering. Mental holds we placed through conditioned thinking, domestication, and environmental influences. If we're practicing consciousness, mental holds shouldn't exist. We shouldn't paint a picture in our minds to have a grasp on our capacity to move forward and think more positively through lessons. We need to be present to recognize the ego.

Our created barriers of depth by the ego can create unhappiness. Often, we go through life without realizing that the extent of our being is not present and not understand the root of our grief. We will operate on the surface (i.e., job, possessions, identity in society) without allowing the depth of our being to foster. I strongly encourage taking the quality time to get to know yourself and introduce your many dimensions to your existence. There is no reason to suppress your happiness.

Suppress

In your current state of being, how would you describe your emotional state? Be honest and articulate with your response. You may reveal room for growth in your current emotional state.

Emotional negativity may exist in your current state. The expression will be apparent through your view of people and reality. You'll continually find the worst in people without the knowledge of their actual being, as speaking negatively about others, become a sport. Who can say the worst thing about a person funnily to arouse laughter to the audience? Or maybe it's an emotional outlet to express all the negativity on your mind, to no longer think about it? When does it stop? Once we recognize that the expression of negativity about others is our unconscious projection of internal negativity.

There is a self-division issue in society. People tend to want to be around others for connection yet still feel empty in the relationship. There is a fear of being alone with yourself. We instead surround ourselves with people, feel disconnected than be alone, and connect. When will we make this self-connection and thrive in humanity without fear? We divide because of distance with ourselves and the world of humanity. We achieve closeness through awareness and without conditions. Mindfulness will close the gap of division. I no longer create division, as I focus on closing the gap within to bring closeness in my environments. I encourage you to be one with your authentic self and the universe. Regain your connection with your soul and the soul of others; we interconnect with each other. Self-division can no longer be the cause of our unhappiness.

Does a lack of internal happiness seep out in your day to day life? Do loneliness and dissatisfaction continuously take control of your life? The feeling of not being enough is the byproduct of internal unhappiness. You may feel there is no sense of direction and foundation in life to remove you from this state. You find yourself trying to compensate in other areas to feel fulfilled.

Do you feel you're enough? Does this feeling consume your being?

Loneliness is a frame of mind and mental attitude toward your environment. Most times, we create an idea of isolation in our minds even when surrounded by people that love us. It is an illusion serving the ego to isolate ourselves from our authentic power. In a state of isolation, your mind fills with dark thoughts, and there is no clarity. You may tend to remain in unfavorable conditions to avoid the idea of being alone. This tendency forces your inner consciousness to diminish. In times of loneliness, remember love prevails, and clearing your mind of egoic thoughts will set you free.

If you're feeling lonely, find a way to connect deeper with yourself to reduce the impact on your being. The gap between you and your authentic self is the root. The more profound connection with yourself keeps you grounded in any situation. Always remember you're never alone when love is forever flowing in the universe. Make sure you're in the space to receive frequencies of love.

Our frequencies can get in the way of love and happiness. Be comfortable expressing the emotions you're feeling. We are domestic to suppress our feelings when we endure discomfort or pain. Any thought or feeling you have is a form of energy! We can create negative energy through suppression and internal distress. The creation of negative energy may project onto your environment.

Prayer or devotion to ease internal unhappiness:

Higher power (inner being),

I ask for guidance to bring more happiness in my life and end my internal suffering. I'm willing to begin and continue the interior work needed to achieve internal gratification. Cultivating unconditional love for myself and living a compassionate life will reduce the production of any unhappy feelings. I know this journey will take some time and effort, but I'm willing to commit along with your guidance to keep me on the right path. I surrender myself to love and happiness.

Commit to this prayer or devotion for connection without attachment!

Express

What are some emotions produced from attachment? Some emotions that quickly come to mind: worry, stress, sadness, impatience, hate, and anger. All these emotions derive from fear, which is the root of all negative emotions. Fear can take many forms without being easily identifiable. The recognition of fear in our life makes us examine our experiences and acknowledge how we promote our attachment to emotions.

But what is attachment? A self-created idea of permanence through a weak bond to a person or thing.

The bond can take different shapes: physical, mental, or emotional with a surface level context or deep roots. Physically, by always wanting to be with a person or in their space, not allowing alone time for either party. Mentally, by taking on a person's thoughts or always putting their needs before yours. Emotionally, by not putting yourself first while allowing yourself to attach to a person's feelings. These different shapes of attachment do not bring you close to your authentic self; it pushes you away. Many experiences can lead to attachment, including not giving the desired attention to growing up or the dependence on another person to feel whole or complete. As you progress through life, you'll push the feelings you created in your past on present situations unconsciously.

Possessiveness stimulates attachment making it difficult to let something go. Your identification with people and things shows attachment. Identification with anything can be uneasy with the loss, so we must not allow our unconsciousness to lead this action. We must be conscious of this possessive behavior.

Do you feel like you need another person to be complete? Our creation into this universe was as whole beings. When did you become reliant on another person to feel complete? To feel incomplete, hoping to create a whole situation is an oxymoron. If you don't feel full, you'll always find yourself in incomplete situations. Attachment leads to deception. The three P's deceives you:

- Pleasure—the internal enjoyment with the condition to be in another person's life.
- Permanence—the lasting perception of the situation with the condition to not see an end.
- Pain—the unpleasant experience with the condition to ignore your internal damage.

We hold onto an optimistic view of the three, which creates attachment. The common thing between all three Ps is that they are all temporary. Nothing is permanent; pain and pleasure are temporary.

Is there a connection between attachment and vulnerability? By not developing attachment prevent vulnerability? There is a connection between the two concepts. Being attached to someone doesn't make you closer to someone; it masks your insecurities and suffering. Attachment allows you to shift the attention needed on yourself and focus on something or someone else. It prevents you from focusing on yourself and putting your actual needs first. Real vulnerability starts with being honest with yourself and being willing to express your true self. Attachment is an issue because it shows dishonesty with yourself. The acknowledgment of attachment reveals deeper internal issues. If you're not vulnerable with yourself, how can you be vulnerable with another person? Attachment in any way is unhealthy and uncorrelated to vulnerability. Attachment extends our suffering, and vulnerability promotes healing.

You will become powerless by feed the ego your power through attachment. Give up all attachments and bring forth your higher self. There is no reason to hold on to any attachments in your evolution of consciousness.

Let's talk about the idea of taking something personally. It's an intuitive concept that takes understanding that you are not involved in the personal matters of another. To not take things personally is crucial when dealing with a person at a different level of awareness. Your enact ability to remove yourself and be a service of compassion for others creates a sense of empathy. It's easy to take something personally when the ego is present. There is self-protection by not taking things personally.

There are many negative emotions tied to the idea of taking something personally. The use of positive emotions, such as love and compassion for a person, will counteract negative emotions. If necessary, withdraw from a situation in the best interests of a person and yourself. Self-work and shift of perspective keep us from taking matters personally. Self-work is removing conditions from your mind to see your authentic self in the universe. Self-work comes with responsibility.

Are you taking responsibility for your feelings? Don't allow your emotions to consume your life. Create emotional boundaries within yourself to manage your energy. Emotional boundaries not only help us to have healthy relationships with others but also help us with a healthy relationship with ourselves. It's essential to set these boundaries to safeguard yourself from emotional manipulation and pain. Welcome your feelings, but refrain from allowing your energy to identify with those feelings. Your unconsciousness will enable you to identify negative emotions. It's essential to acknowledge any traumas feeding on the strength of your existence and mental capacity. Become available to yourself and reflect your greatness in the universe. Emotional boundaries become critical in taking responsibility.

Our reluctant behavior to take responsibility for our emotions has an impact on social behavior in society. Why is there a faster reaction to negativity than to positivity? Why is that our social norm?

Why do we conform to social norms? How are you challenging the normalcy in society? Some ways I challenge social norms are by questioning, redefining, and assessing impact in my life. Be the creator of your reality. By allowing social normality to affect your personal experience without thinking, you bring great disservice to your progress and perception of the truth.

Perceive

The difference between pain and suffering is time. Pain is short-lived, and we can eradicate it from our life more easily. Suffering is long-lived and manifested from the ego. The ego does not want suffering to end; instead, it creates depth and makes our existence unmindful.

The remedy of pain and suffering is your authentic self. The more we evolve, the light of our authentic self grows, making it difficult to internalize these concepts of pain and suffering. Keep in mind our authentic power is far greater than the ego.

Let's add some context and talk about one of the biggest fears in society: infidelity. The internal fear projected onto partners. Cheating is the willingness to be intimate in any way with another person while in commitment. We must acknowledge the act that infidelity lies with the personal ego. It's important not to internalize an action; you don't have the power to prevent engagement. In the commitment, we must be responsible for ourselves instill trust in our partners.

If you don't have full faith in your partner, do you have confidence in your partner? It's crucial to get to know your partner, be aware of who they are in the present moment, and make continuous efforts to communicate your feelings —our confidence in an individual stem from our understanding of their being. We must ask ourselves after the act of infidelity: can you stay in a healthy relationship with impaired trust? The focus of this question is about your happiness and service to your authentic being.

Forgiveness takes place after you've acknowledged and accepted the fact it had nothing to do with your greatness. Betrayal can be intentional and unintentional; there can be betrayal with purpose and malice, but it can also be betrayal without regard to ill will and consideration of impact. Intentions are clear with honesty. While confidence affects the relationship, attachment to the idea can set up to pain and suffering. Refrain from attaching your trust to people or things. Think about the removal of that thing or person, would you feel more or less confident? Assigning your attributes to people or situations through attachment reveals insecurities.

Reliance on a partner can open up insecurities about yourself. The dependency on your partner masks your insecurities instead of addressing your uncertainties. There should be a focus on learning and connecting with yourself in any relationship. To be present with your partner, you must first be present with yourself. Our self-respect plays a role in insecurities and our ability to be present.

Do you disrespect yourself yet get offensive when someone disrespects you? The ego empowers you to disrespect yourself while using the same power to protect against any disrespect from others. To berate yourself daily and get angered when someone else attempts to tear you down reflects emotional suffering. You try to attack someone for having the same thoughts you have about yourself and pointing out the insecurities that your mind mirrors every day.

What does self- respect look like to you? Self-respect is a code of conduct in ourselves and our being in humanity. Emotional healing must take place to value ourselves with respect, setting the standard for others to appreciate our self-value and respect our nature. On the other side, people may not honor you from their level of self-respect, but we must not allow their attempt to devalue, take us to the attack level and stroke power of the ego. Don't take things personally, respect yourself, respect others, and stop emotional suffering.

Often, there are attempts to justify poor treatment to others by the belief that reciprocating the treatment you received will make you feel better. The harmful goal of making someone feel what you've felt is to use poor treatment as a way to get back to someone. Everyone should treat others with love and kindness regardless of our internal reactions to external situations. We do ourselves a disservice by holding on to things and inflicting pain onto others. The immediate response from a place of anger and negativity is counterproductive to our peace of mind. All situations don't deserve a reaction, and the sooner we realize that the better off we'll be in the world of humanity: our anticipation of reacting clouds thought and decisive answers to situations. The way forward is a mindful reaction to the situation and the willingness to spread love unconditionally regardless of receiving unfavorable treatment.

Our minds condition into believing another person

grants our freedom from certain emotions. Why don't we allow our liberty? Do other people have more say in our lives? Often, we use external beings to mask our internal feeling. We have the power and capacity for liberation. Be sure to check freedom to any situation and be open to learning for your betterment.

How do you learn to find internal and external forgiveness from hurt?

- The first step would be the acknowledgment of the felt hurt and understand your internal ties to the experience. This step takes honesty to uncover the root of your pain. Most times, the damage stems internally, and the external circumstance reveals that soft spot.
- The second step would be to forgive yourself. This step involves accountability in choices made and releases any resentment from those choices. There is a need for accountability in any decisions made.
- The third step would be to forgive the person, and this takes patience and time. This step involves a direct or indirect approach. This is the process of self-expressed forgiveness or in-house forgiveness of the circumstance. This step is crucial as it gives power back to our state of presence and permission to move forward.

It's essential to keep in mind that forgiveness is not a blame game of fault; it's a spiritual practice to reduce any hindrance to your present state.

This spiritual practice includes the effort to redefine forgiveness from your perspective. Refrain from subscribing to others' definitions of forgiveness for your healing. There is no set remedy on forgiveness as each person has a distinct view on the matter. The impact of mercy on a person's life may vary, but you have to remember to be honest with your feelings and thoughts as there is healing in truth.

Try this exercise: make a list of people who have or could hurt you. The people on this list have the power of hurting, including your unconscious self. Restrain from giving your power to not identify with hurt to anybody on this list. Possibly, people on this list can physically hurt you, but, emotionally and mentally, they can't do it without your permission. In life, be able to acknowledge if any hurt impacts your freedom.

Sometimes, it's easy to leave a situation when things are going well because it gives your ego a safe exist. Though, it becomes difficult to leave a situation that's a dead-end when things are not going well as the ego takes over. After all, your ego becomes comfortable and neglects your true feelings as this façade of control distorts reality.

On a deeper level, this falsified reality even comes up in death. Do you think about some underlying emotions besides grief when a loved one passes away? Death takes a hard hit due to personal reasons through perception. The actual passing of the person is secondary, as the unsolved emotions felt maybe a source of the relationship with the person.

After death, the carry-over of feelings shows up as a way to release or resent non-expression. The ego often takes advantage of vulnerable moments to seek an understanding of something clear. Efforts made to make sense of a natural event that aligns with the life cycle. The struggle is with acceptance or unwillingness to accept death for personal reasons. We should avoid taking anything personal, including death, as its part of the Divine's will. Our power during times of death comes from our wisdom, the consideration outside of the act being a personal attack, but an opening for growth.

Life aims for the evolution of our authentic being, don't allow the ego to get in the way of getting help in this process. The first part of getting help is the willingness to receive support. The second part is holding yourself accountable and trusting that any difficult moment will pass.

If you are not willing to receive help and resist, you will not create the capacity to hold yourself accountable and trust the process of raising awareness in your life. The real power of help is you! You contain all the answers if you're open to surrendering to your authentic being and accepting the truth. Don't allow expectations of the ego to stunt your growth.

Observe

Most times, disappointment comes from expectations. Be aware of any expectations, both internally and externally, including the drivers of meeting those expectations. Often as a child, I would put my expectations of model parents onto my parents. This habit caused moments of resentment. I was continuously disappointed due to my expectations. These expectations were not theirs, and it was unfair for me to push my expectations or visions of what parents should or shouldn't do. There was equal resentment between both parents. One was no better or worse than the other. I never expressed my expectations verbally but in-house mentally. I was micromanaging my parent's best from personal expectations.

This conditioned behavior followed me, and I continuously pushed my expectations to individuals. I would never exhibit judgment as I never considered myself perfect, but I would expect the absolute best from an individual as I always delivered at any moment. Again, this was not fair. My realization allowed me freedom. I no longer focus on pushing my expectations on others but staying true to my expectations. At any moment, other people's best effort is true to their level of awareness. My concern redirects to myself, and I became more compassionate for others that way. There was great appreciation through this realization.

Be mindful of the ego in any expectations you set. Are your expectations pure from your authentic self or impure from the ego? Often without expectations, we ran into the problem of being unintentional due to the fear of expectations and outcome not in our favor. We must not fear expectations and shouldn't identify with them either. There is an act of intentionality in setting expectations. It's acceptable to have expectations, but the ability not to attach oneself to outcomes, not to consume oneself with the expectations you have set, or to push one's expectations onto others, is the way to liberation.

Mindfulness influences our feelings. Emotions stem from the mental configuration of our instincts, and you feel through this idea; the internal registration of our current state of mind and awareness. We think emotions and create reactions internally and externally from our beliefs of senses. Feelings can be inauthentic from the ego or authentic from our spirit. Our feelings can have conditions, which will create a reaction based on the conditioning of our mind. Consciousness helps us decipher where our feelings are coming from and apprehend the true essence.

How are you managing the energy in your life? Are you confining yourself to energy fields in your environment, or are you surrendering to the creation of your energy force field? The conscious practice of not absorbing energy but acknowledging it exists whether it's negative or positive. The production of your power and responsibility for your energy in this universe help manage your emotions and feelings.

It's easy to feel disconnected from your true self when you're in adverse environments and around hostile people, as this unknowingly creates a blockage in the positive flow of energy in your space. In these situations, it's vital to protect your space and allow your natural positive flow of energy through your body emit in the universe. Do not enable environments or people to dictate your freedom. Do not be a victim of unconsciousness.

Often, we confuse empathy with the absorption of emotion. Empathy is the awareness of other emotions and understanding with knowledge but does not mean for you to take on those emotions. The created empathic insight through the channel of our intuition and lived experiences. Be mindful at the moment, and do not make someone else story your story.

Emotional awareness is essential in any relationship. It allows us to use empathic abilities to manage relationships with ourselves and others. We create an understanding of our emotions through awareness. The benefits of this will show up in the way we communicate our feelings, understand other people's emotions, resolve emotional distress, and handle conflict.

Accept and question your emotions. All emotions are valid; this is where acceptance comes into play. We should examine the reason for feeling the emotions to discover the root. Our recognition of triggers not only help our well-being but, begin our healing process. Inquisition puts us in a place of service to ourselves.

Release

In conjunction with the service to ourselves, it brings the idea of reverence. But what is reverence? The heartfelt respect for people and things. Allow reverence to take place in your lives. This concept defines externally, but it has a high context internally. The profound respect we have for someone or something should be a mirror of our being. There should never be any disconnection of respect. The saying goes, "treat others as you want to be treated"—the universal concept of connection we need to practice.

Encourage your mind to produce more positive emotions to bring value to your life. We need to support each other to feel positive emotions such as love, happiness, and peace. Having a good relationship with yourself will promote a good relationship with others; extend your positivity.

In moments of adversity, the acknowledgment of negative emotions reveals areas to expand to higher frequencies. Learn to transform unfavorable conditions into positive shifts in your life. We can overcome any adversity with willpower and confidence in our abilities. We must accept it's acceptable to take a break and re-center yourself. The break can be two hours, one day, weekend, or whatever time you need to recollect yourself for the greater good of any situation.

Today let go of any emotion you've been struggling with as it roots by fear. I encourage you to live fearlessly and deal with that emotion head-on! Always be clear about your feelings even when you're uncomfortable saying them out loud. Step out of your comfort zone and leap into honesty with what you feel. There is so much strength in self-vulnerability that immerse in captivity.

Do you believe emotions are infections? The idea of energy transference holds for emotions if the person allows. We sometimes feel this when bad energy is present from someone's feelings and thoughts.

Let's create energy transference in positive habits and outlook, the ability to inspire a shift of action by exemplifying those very things. Closeness to yourself and interactions with other people can make this transfer process faster. The goal is never to change someone, but to be the change and other teams will happen simultaneously. Energy transfers easily, and our bodies become receptive of all energies. Allow your shift to a positive habit; in reality, open your mind.

Reflect

1. What are some things that make you smile?
2. Complete the sentence: my energy is most abundant when...
3. What are your biggest stress drivers? What are the causes of these drives?
4. List members of your support system
5. It's important to acknowledge all aspects of any situation. What is preventing you from seeing the positive aspects of any situation? Why do you feel inclined to only focus on the negative aspects of situations?

4

MIND

"True happiness relates more to the mind and heart."—Dalai Lama.

I magine jumping into a large body of water with an endless supply of oxygen and discovering the things that you were only able to find. It's like building up your mental abilities with awareness, patience, and commitment. We have unlimited capabilities, and the power to uncover an endless supply of knowledge.

Our ignorance is prolonging our suffering in our egoic state of mind. We refrain from seeking knowledge to complete understanding due to fear. We've become, so content with conditional thinking that our psyche to explore positive thinking frightens us. The goal is to expand awareness to end suffering.

There is deception in believing we cannot remove conditions and live a life without conditions. This deceit is furthest from the truth. The mental ability to hone in on awareness and love eradicates any response to conditioning. This shift all begins with the ignition of our authentic power that lights our inner ambition to be our highest self without limitations.

Limit

When will we let our false self die? Why do we continue to hold on? It's due to our created attachments, fear of the unknown (all we know is our false self), and conditioned thinking built throughout our life. Self-labels inject us with a perception of a false self. We label ourselves due to conditioning from ourselves and others.

The difference between self-centered and to center in self: the level of consciousness. Self-centered calls for unconsciousness that ignores the universe around you and only acknowledges your unawareness. There is a lack of spiritual connection in self-centeredness. Focusing on yourself requires knowledge that recognizes the present moment while at the same time maintaining peace with your inner self. Centering self involves going to the core of your inner being and connecting with the spiritual world.

There is a need to explore the spiritual and therapeutic vocabulary to express how we feel. Most times, people don't explain how they feel because they're unable—not having the appropriate words and clarity to voice inner feelings. People only understand from their place of awareness. Instead of learning or seeking understanding, we attach ourselves to that level of knowledge. Let's remember compassion should drive any moments of unawareness to see things from different lenses. Shift how you express yourself—be mindful and reciprocate how others address you.

Most impaired or partial have no desire to heal and be

whole. Personal revelations start the idea of healing. Will-ingness must happen to open your mind. Surrender to the idea of healing and wholeness. Begin cleaning, sewing, and patching your deep wounds. A partial being is not open to this idea as it sounds impossible to heal from the past and removed from conditions. A conditioned mind of an incom-plete being will go back to the default framework of think-ing. Openness seems unlikely due to fear, but if you counter that with the love of self and compassion toward wholeness, that fear will be obsolete.

Before my state of awareness, I confined my capacity to be vulnerable, which closed off my real power. My ability to share insight and inspire healing is how I can provide service to the universe.

This perception was only possible by dropping my guard and revealing the real thoughts I've held onto due to the associated emotions with the ideas. I wasn't ready to show this part of myself and become susceptible to hurt. I've learned that when someone makes themselves vulnerable, they become available to hurt. I've had an easy way of controlling my emotions to block sensitive spots in my being.

But, I didn't acknowledge that there were real strengths and unimaginable power in being vulnerable. External power can be superficial without any depth beyond the surface. Internal power has a great extent, with the ability to reshape our reality. My openness to vulnerability has been the accelerator of my healing. My spiritual being is guiding my intentions and efforts toward enlightenment. It took real courage for me to be vulnerable. The courage came from my authentic self to move away from my false self.

It's possible to stunt your growth by not asking: what do you want in life?

An internal realization must take place to remove the conditions. This awareness will happen through wisdom. The goal is not to reprogram the mind with new conditions but, remove all conditions and attachments to the false self. You are opening your mind to be unconditional and closing off conditioned thinking.

For example, the conditions of insufficient money and unabundant attitude influence the tendency for people to reach for wealth from a monetary standpoint. This sense of attainment does not hold once received, as satisfaction goes unfulfilled. The happiness once sought out through money, turn out to be conditional. Happiness is still in question. We all want to be happy! But for everyone, that looks different. What is certain is that money does not fix everything. Consciousness is necessary for self-realization. From the soul, we are all rich, and our actual being is abundant and happy.

Often, we capture external possessions as part of our identity. There is a need to separate attachment from these possessions. We even capture our body as our identity. We must refrain from identifying ourselves with our body. The truth is our body is a vessel for our soul and should not be mistaken for our being.

Is it possible to redefine "truth" for ourselves? Yes, it's possible through openness, willingness, and mindfulness. Sometimes we allow one experience to dictate the course of our life. We make decisions that impact our ability to learn and to grow. How are you regulating your mind and spirit? Are you allowing your mind to conquer your spirit desires? Or are you allowing both to flourish in conscious harmony?

When you see fear or suffering around you, this is what you resonate with in life. Fear and suffering become normal. In turn, it prevents you from seeing eternal love and happiness. An unconscious being attracts fear and doesn't inquire within the spirit.

Inquire

Why do we try so hard to align ourselves with a prescribed representation? There is conditioning at a young age to be who our parents or guardians wanted us to be. We made efforts to break away or confine to these expectations, but we never wanted to disappoint. So, we try to conform to the vision of others. We are responsible for our lives and have no accountability for the ideas of others. Be able to recognize, acknowledge, and own this conditioned behavior to open our minds and push forward.

Are you living in the perception of someone else? Regain that power and commit to being who you are without the pressure of a created image by someone else. Don't make someone else story your story!

For me, it was never conditioning myself to an image of my parents but, an ideal image of myself. I push myself to be the best in every way, shape, or form. This push was not an external competition but an internal competition with myself. I used to stress my body and mind out due to my expectations. I focused on the execution of my goals, so sleep wasn't a priority. I was still able to exert a lot of energy due to my natural upbeat personality. To free myself from stress, I left it in 2013.

I committed myself to no longer identify with stress going forward. I no longer suppressed stress in an unhealthy way and the removal of this normal behavior from my life. The removal of fear left me more free from my expectations. When I was able to free myself and come to terms with conditioning, I delivered my best self and did not attach to results. I was able to allow life to run its course and be my best self without attention to a result from my expectations. This part was difficult to fill as I conditioned myself for so long. When there are moments where I see my expectations getting the best of me, I reclaim power and be present to endless possibilities.

If you allow conditioning, it can get in the way of universal awareness, be mindful. Do you have insightful moments provided by the universe? Moments of clear direction and revelation. Often, I have these moments as it relates to spiritual inclination. As I'm moving closer in connection with my spiritual presence, I allow myself to be in the moment to foster clarity and understanding. Also, these insightful moments call for a time of reflection. I'm no longer allowing the ego to control moments of discovery.

Discovery is leading to complete learning and understanding. The best way to learn is to give up any pre-existing beliefs and give attention to the existing content. This surrender will allow you to remove conditioning of the mind and learn without conditions through openness. Put an end to fragmentation in learning. Open your mind and make connections to the overarching goal of knowledge, which is to expand our minds for awareness. You can hinder your awareness through ignorance and fragmented learning. This process is learning through piece mail with no real understanding of the content.

Opinions can give an understanding of an individual thought process and awareness. We can learn through views when the perspective is clear. Everyone has their idea, and that opinion comes from personal perception. Internal understanding must take place to eliminate the constraints. It's not a matter of agreeing or disagreeing but, being present to the expression at the moment. We express opinions can verbally and nonverbally. So be present and aware of learning through acceptance.

Acceptance comes without attachment to an idea of what it was or what it should be. Recognition mirrors the present state of things. There is an agreement with understanding through acceptance. Why do situations have to hit home for us to be accepting and show compassion in understanding? Some examples of concepts: sexuality (specifically homosexuality), gender identity (specifically transgender), addiction (precisely drugs and alcohol), and race (specifically marriage of different races and befriending a different race). These are all concepts our immediate family and friends remain ignorant to until a loved one resonates with one of the ideas. The education on any subject improves our comprehension, promoting love, acceptance, and compassion. We are afraid of what we don't fully understand. We must drive away from our fear of our unknown and face it with awareness.

For example, addiction has to do with mental disparity. The use of things to escape reality and numb the pain produce from identification with circumstances. This disparity invaded my family members. The abnormality in behavior was evident through observation. But, the unconscious mind blinded these members from awareness.

We create what we see. Our mind creates visuals based on our perception of things. This idea is the reason why people don't always see the same thing. Also, our opinions are different, which creates our reality of things. The idea that perception is reality stems from the conditioning of lived experiences. We identify or make things real in our minds to comprehend the world. Perception does not always consider intuition. Sometimes it's like they're moving in parallel. Attitude can drive the ego, while the soul drives intuition. We allow the ego to create impressions of things in the universe by using our mind as a vessel for control. Never silence your intuition and remain in power.

Our intuition is without fear and pure. Rediscover the truth in our lives and release fear and hate produced by the ego.

Challenge

Challenge your existing beliefs. Are you stuck in time? Do you feel like your thoughts have not moved with time? It's because you've harvested that energy, which prevents you from moving forward. So, harness the power of intention because, through it, you can create new thoughts. We attach to our beliefs without knowing. Sometimes our opinions are all we know due to our ignorance of other views and perspectives. This tendency can come off as being stuck in your way because you're unwilling to listen or consider new ideas.

Can you detach from one single belief? What is the display of this idea of detachment? The opening of our mental capacity to learn and appreciate different perspectives on the same concept. Religion is one of the most common topics that people struggle with due to their inability to accept new thoughts or teachings. No one has to identify with a religion to understand the concept. Also, the free will to resonate with varying beliefs through comprehension is acceptable. I have studied other religions to complete my awareness: Zoroastrianism, Jainism, Humanism, Baha'i, Buddhism, Hinduism, Jehovah's Witness, Unitarianism, Paganism, Taoism, Christianity, and Islam.

We should expand our knowledge of all religions. The decision to adopt a belief system or not should come from your understanding, not conditioning to a single belief(s). The point is to be well informed. These are strides to remove attachment and domestication in our daily lives. It's all right to research different religions; it's not considered immoral. We do ourselves a disserve by not being well-informed and aware of various beliefs in the universe.

Religion derives from spirituality. Religion without principles of spirituality is like practicing with no purpose. There is a groundedness in spirituality. Spirituality is not separate from life; it is an inclusive lifestyle. With any belief system, you pick and choose what will serve your life. In a sense, religion is self-servicing, while the principles apply to anyone's life. Practices being subjective, with selective reasoning, to live by all practices, or to live by specific methods.

In many religions, the act of sharing the message has transformed into acceptance in a community. The invitation of all does not hold. The selectivity distorts the real message of faith, enlightenment, and presence. We often have seen people runaway or fear religion for these reasons. One of the biggest things in humanity is acceptance, and religion has put a great divide in people and the true meaning of acceptance. There is the conditioning of misrepresenting religious ideals. Principles to include all and create oneness is now an example of selective agreement. We must close the gap, accept all, and allow enlightenment into the teachings. But learning is often distorted by human conditioning and ego, which causes misinterpretation.

As a person brought up in Christian faith, I've seen first-hand how the church can judge and not send a warm invitation to people trying to receive the word. I can stand here today as a more enlightened individual and not resonate with one religion and observe an Omnist point of view. Our relationship with religion should be in alignment with our understanding.

I have taken time to understand different faiths and compare the principles of their belief systems. I realized religions have overarching themes in common, yet we create division. Acceptance is always at the forefront as it pertains to understanding the faith. The superiority of beings is often obsolete through the teaching of religion. So why is it so easy to judge and not accept? The ego has invaded teachers of religion.

In religion, we need to be aware of judgment and respect for healing from suffering. The healing process becomes complicated when judgment is present. This immoral act may hinder a person from healing and prolonging their suffering through resentment. As one of the solid principles of most religions, enlightenment, is complete without the essence of judgment.

We have to close the gap of separation and educate ourselves while loving each other. No one should feel alienated due to personal beliefs. We must uncover our views and not judge others for their faith. How the saying goes: Love thy neighbor.

While we're all spiritual beings, even though spiritual principles and practices may not guide us. I'm not playing checkers; I'm playing chess with consciousness and unconsciousness. The multitude of this battle is far greater than what most of us realize. This fight has been going on for centuries, the struggle of the ego. We win this battle by pushing ourselves into a state of consciousness. The art of being present in unconscious environments is the art of war. As you move toward higher consciousness, you can't allow any unconscious act or word to hinder your goal and disserve progress. Let go and let the Divine order handle it.

Enhance your brain. Continue to learn, process, and apply knowledge in your life. Never limit yourself to current knowledge and always be willing to further your intelligence. How to create new thoughts? Challenge and question any pre-existing beliefs, evaluate and reflect on its existence in your life.

New

Foster your curiosity. Be open to exploring all the universe has to offer, expanding your knowledge, and creating all the experiences that serve your being in the direction of greatness. We grow through openness and unexpected strays from our passion. The deviations from our passion create character and new perspectives. Don't abandon your true passion; find ways to keep it relevant in your life without restricting your curious mind to experience new things.

Recite this:

My unconsciousness will not win anymore! I will continue to foster consciousness as I become closer to enlightenment, eternal happiness, and peace.

Be a curious student in your life:

- Acknowledge the progression in your life.
- Continuously learn.
- Grow from experiences.
- Build meaningful relationships.
- Seek guidance from practitioners (i.e.,

individuals who have understanding and
practice daily).

This correlation of being a student is significant, as one day, you will be the master of your life, which is only possible by learning yourself and your purpose in the universe.

The nature of our thinking process influences our learning. Are you opening your minds to divergent thinking during problem-solving? What is divergent thinking? It's brainstorming that utilizes our creativity to produce ideas and potential explanations to solve an issue. In this state of thinking, you're not using logic; you're using creativity to develop solutions. This free-thinking allows our mind to think outside of the box with intention. Divergent thinking can help us answer many issues we have in our daily lives and the universe.

How is the concept of evolution different through mental openness in thought? We often see evolution as being progressive, but you can look at it as going back to what we have always been—whole. Understanding the way of evolution is reverting to our original state, which is complete and limitless. We're never shifting into something we were never but, shifting our mind and beingness back to its authentic state. You can view evolution as linear and nonlinear by defining it through perception. Look at development through a transformative lens. There is nothing secular about evolution.

Feed your mind, feed your spirit. Free your mind, body, and soul from captivity! Allow your authentic self to manifest openness and wisdom. Whatever no longer serves you, let it go!

Reflect

1. Think about your belief system and how your beliefs impact your life. How do the core principles of spirituality (i.e., love, compassion, interconnectedness, acceptance, fearlessness, etc.) play a part in your beliefs?
2. Write down your deepest secret(s). Describe the secret, how you felt/ feel, and why it's a secret?
3. What are three words to describe your state of being?
4. Make it your duty today to find a book that resonates with your state of mind and begin to read.
5. How can you create a healthy perspective fueled with higher consciousness and the absence of ego?

SECTION TWO

Opening of a conscious soul

His consciousness is ever-evolving.

5

AWARENESS

"Awareness is the greatest agent for change."—Eckhart Tolle.

Mindfulness is an internal commitment to every act of life. Mindfulness plays a part in healing. What is healing? Healing has internal and external contexts relating to recovery. True healing begins inside to outside. Healing starts with yourself.

I'm going to focus on the internal framework of healing from the soul perspective. What is the soul? The soul is our authentic being inside our body, which connects us to our higher power, the Divine. The recovery of our authentic self has significance to living a life not consumed by the ego. We must expel unconsciousness, conditioned thinking, and domestication created by our environments.

When are we going to decide to heal? Today, in this present moment. We're going to be receptive and make a difference in our lives now!

Healing can be uncomfortable when you're learning

about yourself! People avoid remediation of their issues to remain comfortable in their current state of mind. When It comes to healing, you have to go deep to the cut. You may have to revisit the cut a few times and not leave behind a scar. Emotional healing it's imperative. When you can understand and have the ability to articulate your feelings, it is when you begin to feel the influence of emotional healing that is vital to your consciousness. Start with family and early social environments for healing! Be a positive shift in your family and surroundings. Be the one that you see as your true self.

There are pessimistic reactions to therapy and healing in our society. Following this idea: "It won't work." Let's encourage more today, especially when someone is manifesting suffering in their life. Don't play victim to societal views, seek the help needed in your life. Transform your connection to thoughts and feelings with conditions. Allow the shifts without conditions to be in harmony with your higher power as a spiritual being. Don't conform to societal responses that surrounded you growing up—be open to guidance, love yourself, and reunite with your true nature.

Conditioning has built walls keeping us from our authentic self. We now have to knock down those barriers and reunite with our unlimited power, our soul. Separation has been going on for years, but now is the time to reconnect with your inner self, and the power you once felt was external. Self-realizing that power was internal all along!

Awareness comes with knowledge and application. One of the biggest questions in our universe: how to be more conscious? To be present. Understanding mindfulness has a spiritual context that plays a part in the holistic idea of consciousness. Remove the division of things in your life.

Live free! Stop making excuses for different people, situations, and thoughts.

Think about your consciousness being on sleep mode; this is our reality. Be fully present in every moment because every moment passes. The idea of reverting to the past is non-existent. We must take each moment and display the presence of our authentic self.

Authentic

Our connection to our higher power and the Divine is through the soul. Be aware of your energy, emotions, feelings, and thoughts that produce in every moment. The positive energy produced from smiling can give us a closeness to the connection of higher power.

Smile more! Nothing should prevent you from exhibiting radiance in the world. There is always something to smile about and give internal appreciation. Be more conscious of the times when you're not smiling, and rejoice! There is no cost to smile, but there is a toll on your attitude and demeanor when you don't exercise smiling. There is no reason not to reinforce our genuine connection with the universe.

Will you choose to make a shift in your presence?

In my eyes, a self-aware person is influential; the fullness of awareness on both the non-spiritual and spiritual levels. The use of introspective and extrospective lenses in presence is extraordinary. The power to be authentic in looking within yourself and around your surroundings without the ego. So, what is power? This term is subjective and based on individual perspective. For me, knowledge is power, and the ability to apply that knowledge is influential.

Through self-discovery, I've acknowledged that there are two forms of knowledge: internal and external. This is the intimate understanding of your authentic self, soul, and external knowledge of the surrounding universe. The acquisition of both takes willingness, honesty, openness, examination, and application. There are no such things as useless knowledge. All information plays a part in the synchrony of beings and our expressions of evolution.

Is our power drawn from our physical identity or spiritual identity? How do you acknowledge your power? Our influence should never be superficial, as this is a temporary illusion until there is a calling for clarity. Our energy should always be authentic, as this is enduring with reality. Some examples of real power are groundedness, centeredness, unity, service, and positive influence in the universe.

Follow these words with me:
I feel free to be myself.
I feel unconditional love.
I feel happy.

Acceptance comes from self-acceptance, presence, nonjudgment, sincerity, condition less, and no expectation of satisfaction from anyone or anything. What are your plans for acceptance? My plan for self-acceptance is to be more conscious and escape the realm of unconsciousness. This acceptance means more love, compassion, and mindfulness. Always keep compassion in mind. We should never overlook compassion as it is a staple in the evolution of humanity.

For your evolution, what are you inspired by within? Think about something that you've always been proud of and the impact it has made in your life. For me, I admire many qualities within myself, but my creative mind continuously inspires me. The ability to allow my creativity to flow through any project or opportunity has been impactful in my life. Creativity plays a part in awareness. For me, creativity is the ability to express oneself in a way that promotes artistic skills and mind therapy while being free from conditions. My creativity has been a form of liberation to set my soul free in moments of expression.

Are you connecting to what you have the desire to do? Explore the importance of pure desire in your life and the impact of consistency. Why does it matter? The connection can transform your experience and provide the fulfillment of desires. Make sure your passion is pure without the ego! Believe in your values and remain grounded. Cherish your values, vision, and goals.

Be in the right condition to allow things to unfold in your life. Most times, we are not in the proper condition to receive because our unawareness has polluted our light to see things consciously. We tend to miss out on signs we asked the Divine for in this state of unawareness. The deliverance of our authentic self will position us to let no longer our ego get in the way of greatness unfolding. What does unfold mean? This means revealing any suppression by the cover of unconsciousness. Uncovering our full potential requires our awareness—diligence to the idea of our higher power. You're powerful!

Is your spiritual state translated into situations and encounters with people? Are you always in survival mode and neglecting self-care? Through practicing self-care, you'll no longer be in survival mode; you'll feel alive and full in spirit. The spirit sources our higher power. The heighten energy emitted from your presence will become a shield to any negativity produced from our environments. Self-confidence fortifies these practices awakening your authentic being.

I resisted vulnerability for so long. I chose to shut down that part off from my authentic being, as this was fear-based but a protective mechanism based on lived experiences. Now, I take my authentic self into my endeavors, not allowing unawareness to define my presence in the universe. I encourage you to become so involved in your life that it brings yourself closer to your authentic self. Be able to look inside your soul and be honest with your actual being. Sift through your relationship with yourself and show genuine interest in getting to know yourself.

Integrate

Be joyful! Joy speaks to the soul. Our body reacts to joy in a fantastic way that promotes an overabundance of positive frequency in our life. Allow the body to experience joy through the presence and absence of the ego. Be more active in our physical well-being. Joy is forever if you allow it to be continuous in your daily life. Allow balance to bring joy and peace in your life. There are joy and peace in the removal of conditions in the mind and body energy.

Feminine and masculine energy needs balance. We should pay more attention to our feminine, and masculine energy as unbalance creates a discrepancy between self and others. The disconnection stops us from being our authentic selves. We are often taught males have masculine energy, and women have feminine energy. This statement is incomplete, as every being have masculine and feminine energy. Human beings may have a heightened flow of one than the other due to their unawareness of the other. The completeness of both energy flow ignites a full being in tune with the properties of expression. Some examples of masculine energy features are logical, reason, action-oriented, and stable, while some of the examples of feminine energy features are intuitive, nurturing, emotional awareness, and expressive. There are many differences in both energy flows, but the connection of both becomes supportive in our higher self. These energy flow can co-exist together in harmony within one being, as awareness and balance are necessary for divinity.

Nature exhibits a perfect balance of feminine and masculine energy. How in tune are you with nature? I'm not just talking about woods, forests, and jungles. I'm talking about mother nature in our everyday life—the bodies of water, trees, flowers, insects, animals, and land around us. Nature has a way of clearing our minds organically. It provides us with thoughts and revelations, but how can we harness this natural energy? Instead of unconscious thoughts, let's create meaningful ideas full of intent and consciousness. Embrace the flow of things provided through nature. We're all one, and we're all connected. Become one with divinity.

How are you filling yourself up? This is the mindful act of giving to enable you to give to others. We must continuously fill our tanks so that we can fill the tank of others in need. Think about the power that affirmations and mantras have on their mind. These phrases or words engage our minds and soul together in harmony. The energy they have is incredible and aid in an individual's healing process.

Affirmations and mantras assist in the removal of toxic reality building through the mind.

Emotional, mental, and physical suffering is the cradle of separation from your spiritual self and the present moment. Through suffering, an internal awakening happens. The needed end is necessary to take you to the next level of evolution:

- The first part of suffering is pain. This pain brings attachment to conditioning. There is a necessary removal of conditions you latched onto as a way of life.
- The second part of suffering is a revelation. You realize that everything happens for a reason. Divine reasoning justifies your opportunity for growth.
- The third part of suffering is healing. You begin to heal through awareness and shifts in perspective.
- The final part of suffering is an internal awakening. This part is the key to your higher power. You endured this cycle of suffering to experience true happiness and joy. It takes an open mind to see the trueness in this state. Dedicate to personal growth to weather through any moments you may experience suffering.

The hold of suffering can lift through intent. How does intention play into accountability for your life? It drives accountability for your thoughts, words, and actions. How often are you accepting responsibility for your actions and words? Do you feel less powerful by taking responsibility for your choices?

In society, the ego has made taking accountability and blame, synonymous, so you refrain from accepting accountability to avoid self-blame. The essential part of any situation is never to blame as things planned out as intended inevitably. The focus should be on accountability for your choices and involvement.

So, are you accepting accountability for your happiness? I'm taking responsibility for my happiness.

Why is alone time always associated with an issue? When will we move away from negative notions of alone time? Be mindful to alone time in our human experience. Strengthen your intuition through quality time with yourself. The development of intuition makes the spiritual voice in your being clear. Continue to surrender to the moment and allow your inner being to guide you through experiences. Silence any thoughts clouding your consciousness with negativity and resistance to presence. Our connection with self recognizes strengthened intuition as the truth to the empowerment of the soul.

Our connection leads to the intuitive insight that reveals internal realizations allowing the soul to speak. The deep insights from our intuition help us move through life with more serenity. A peace of mind that brings agreement with our soul.

Mindfulness plays a significant part in our connection with self. Watch over your thoughts, words, feelings, and actions. Get into the rhythm of things as it pertains to mind, body, and spirit. In other words, catch that beat of life. The opposite of absence is presence. The present moment is a gift. Practice consciousness in the present moment.

Practice

Self-protect yourself by not taking things personally. When you take things personally, you stroke the ego and give it the power to manipulate situations through unconsciousness. We protect ourselves by applying awareness to situations, and understanding nothing is personal as it reflects an individual's perception. We save ourselves agony by not taking things personally.

Shift your reality and leave unconsciousness behind. Be intentional in every way! Be intentional with your thoughts, words, actions, self, relationships, and life. I encourage you to make yourself your LTC (Lifetime Crush), always show appreciation to who you are at this moment, and love yourself! Self-love should never display as vanity but, gratitude and acceptance of your presence.

Every day of gratitude, be sure you give grace—your grace in your intentions and the motives of your true self. Gratitude and grace go together in our efforts to awareness. Keep in mind; pure intentions root in love and compassion. The spirit of gratitude and grace will lead to prosperity in your life.

Moreover, gratitude is like appreciation, and grace is like your movement towards appreciation. Be sure your intentions and motives are clear and speak to your true self. A public figure that emits grace and gratitude is Michelle Obama. Her gratitude for life is evident, and her gracefulness fortifies her appreciation. Many come to be inspired by her alignment and truth of her authentic self.

The goal is stillness in thoughts to be fully present. The connection and interrelation of grace and gratitude will awaken new appreciation. When aligned with your spirit, you move in grace. Are you willing to open yourself up to graceful learning? The ability to appreciate lessons and embrace the reality of situations.

Moreover, moving forward without fear. Sometimes we allow circumstances to get the best of us without opening our eyes to the lesson displayed at the moment. Our awareness to redirect our focus on the teachings of the moment is vital to our forward progress.

The practice of meditation creates a stillness in thoughts. Meditation can be difficult when your unconscious mind is trying to interrupt your stillness. The unconscious mind makes meditation almost impossible without thought. We must silence out the ego and grasp the moment of stillness with our conscious mind. To seize this moment, become one with the present moment and reiterate if needed, affirming phrases to keep you grounded in the still moment.

You can fully embrace meditation experiences when you're doing inner work to clear your mind of the clutter that prevents you from being still. The declutter of egoic feelings and thoughts puts us in a trance and exploits the present moment.

The creation of stillness in your mind and body will open the gates of your spirt. Allowing your soul to embrace all the universe has to offer. This way of life helps resolve any inner conflict by bringing further clarity in the act of awareness. The ability to calm and give mental breaks to the mind is powerful, the detachment from the mind to be in the present moment, and foster mental peace. Allow the detachment from internal and external factors that goes against your conscious being.

After meditation, there is room for reflection in self-realization created from the stillness of the mind. We must exploit these opportunities of silence as they bring clarity to our real power.

I advocate for the implementation of meditation and

prayer in your daily life. Meditation is effortless when you are mindful. Prayer is fruitful when you are intentional. Do you have any current practices of meditation and prayer? Are you allowing your mind to be clear through meditation? Are you allowing your heart to speak during prayer?

I've learned that the combination of both brings clarity to my daily life. Both provide liberation of my soul in moments of action. Meditation and prayer are a time to connect with our center. These are moments to give attention to your well-being through pure mindfulness and intention.

Be aware of the way you pray. Be intentional with your expression. You'll receive what you pray for if you're deliberate and deserve reception at the moment. Take time to think about all the things you pray for and all the things you receive from prayer. If you think long enough, you'll see the connection. The things you receive may not always align with what you want or what pleases you, but it is the ask. Remember to be intentional with your prayer. But with intentionality comes knowing your authentic self, so take some time out to understand what you want. We continuously pray about things hoping for a shift and find out we are unhappy with the Divine response. So, are you receiving what you truly desire, or are you receiving what the ego asked? The ego comes into prayer through the unawareness of our authentic desires. So be mindful in the act of prayer and expand your knowledge of self. Prayer is powerful with awareness.

Often, the basic principle of sounds from vibrations infuses therapeutic properties bring self-awareness. Have you ever considered healing through sound? Sound meditation and therapy, use the vibration of sound to promote healing. For centuries, the use of these practices has an impact on society. We are all beings who move by sounds and find them to be therapeutic; explore this experience. We react positively to vibrations as we naturally emit vibrations through our frequency. Sound meditation allows us to emit our higher frequencies by clearing our minds and freeing our spirit. The piercing vibrations consume our body, promote healing, and awaken our inner consciousness. Expanding our frequency is essential to tuning into our higher power. I've integrated sound meditation and therapy in my daily life. I use chimes and singing bowl to spark my inner Zen. I will admit there is a calmness that the vibrations bring to the mind. I listen to meditation instrumental as a way to relax. I use sleep sounds to sleep (i.e., white noise, waterfall, rainfall, etc.). The combination of sounds in my life has helped with improved sleep, clarity of mind, improved breathing, focus, and calmness.

Let's talk about sleep. Sleep is a time to rest your mind and clear your soul. Your quality sleep changes when your mind is clear. When you stress less, your sleep patterns and mood improve for the upcoming day. There could be preexisting feelings still present, but we must always learn to let yesterday go and focus on now. Your feelings towards sleep shift when you're more centered. When anxiety no longer exists, clarity is essential for the mind to flourish. Heavy thinking before resting is not needed. My quality of sleep improved by:

- Reading at least 30 mins before bed;
- Drinking a hot beverage before bed;
- Soaking in a bath before bed;
- Ensuring clean bed sheets;
- Removing the television from my bedroom;

- Turning off lights or using lights that emit red light (like a salt lamp);
- Putting my phone away at least 30 mins before bed;
- Incorporating sleep sounds (if needed);
- Using aromatherapy through essential oil diffuser and pillow mist.

Clearing your mind promotes breakthrough thoughts of consciousness. Make the effort of keeping mental health in mind for forming freshness in thinking. There is nothing like a clear mind and an open soul. You begin to stop asking for much when you realize that you have all that you need.

What spiritual exercises are you doing to protect your consciousness? How are you disciplining your mind for a higher frequency? For me, meditation, prayer, deep breathing, focused breathing, yoga, and journaling. These all create a flow of energy through the soul, which releases high-frequency to the universe. How disciplined are you in your practices for deeper awareness? Use discipline as a way to respect your commitment. Awareness requires being intentional in your everyday life.

Where is your outlet to release energy? For me, the gym. It allows me to clear my mind, be free, and release any tension in my body. This long-standing activity has been a consistent outlet for me through and after college. I've identified a genuine connection to the gym as it relates to my inner clarity. There are many other benefits I see through the gym, but my sole purpose for engaging in this activity is to clear my mental space.

Do you allow quiet reflection for yourself as it aid in your spiritual freedom?

<u>Free</u>

Spiritual health has a meaningful impact on our life. What does spiritual health look like:

- Becoming more in tune with yourself.
- Enforcing values close to you in your life.
- Discovering your purpose and install it for a life of transcendence.

Our existence in the universe deepens through improving our spiritual health. The cleansing of ego power will create more fruitful experiences in life. Take control over your spiritual health to connect with your authentic self. Create a routine of spiritual practices that resonate with your flow of authenticity to reestablish your spiritual presence. This flow can be establishing some sort of habit, like a day full of self-care and taking time out each day to give back to your spirit. I've learned that a combination of both provides a consistent spiritual high of mindfulness. There are many ways to improve your spiritual health, be willing to explore alternatives, and give presence to the other options.

Give up the unconsciousness to live a more intentional life-rebirth of your authentic self in the universe today.

Generosity is an essential part of our awareness. There are many forms of giving, but I'll highlight spiritual giving as the highest level of generosity. This level involves sharing your spiritual self, which is full of enlightenment—giving to others in service of wisdom through high-frequency coaching. An active increase in happiness and love in other people's life transpires. Fulfilling needs without receiving anything in return (i.e., personal gain or expectations). Faithful spiritual giving has no monetary attachment. You are giving the soul a positive influence, allowing your authentic self to be available for service to reduce the suffering of others. For example, high vibrations of positive energy and a conscious frame of mind can be a form of spiritual giving.

Do you always have your best interest in spirit? If so, you're practicing self-compassion. If not, let's embody this practice to be more compassionate toward our being and spread the power to others. Do you always have the best interest of other people? If so, you're practicing compassion. If not, let's empower this practice and make a better effort to circulate compassion in the universe. People give off vibrations that you quickly identify if you are aware. Emotions show up in the world as energy.

One of the four immeasurable in Buddhist teaching is equanimity. Equanimity is the order of serenity and clarity of spirit. There is an open to the present moment bringing a state of stillness and calmness. Through serenity, there are passive reactions with love and wisdom instead of reactive with fear and ignorance. This reaction includes observing what's going on and how it makes you feel with openness and truth. You're whole regardless of the circumstances with patience. To maintain this state, you must stay grounded spiritually. Eventually, you will awaken your authentic self and move into enlightenment.

Enlightenment does not take the pleasure out of life but fill your life with purpose and meaning, which will promote true happiness and joy. Spiritual awareness is a realization that every being has a soul, and the soul is our authentic being. The acquisition of wisdom opens our minds to the understanding that we are spiritual by nature.

Be your peace of mind in any environment! Allow your spirit to compel positive energy into your life. You cannot become what you already are—greatness. You are just returning to the state of the Divine. You're aligning with your authentic self, and not finding yourself.

Reflect

1. How open are you to inner awareness? What are some steps you can take now to make that shift and get closer to your spiritual being?
2. Write a list of things you are grateful for today.
3. Have you ever taken any of these things for granted?
4. How will you commit to taking better care of yourself today?
5. Self-check yourself. Write some recommendations to improve your presence.
6. When are you most at peace?
7. Complete the sentence: I'm happiest when...
8. How are you managing negative feelings or thoughts before sleep to create a higher state of awareness in your present being?

6
_____

THINK

"Thinking is opening yourself to inside revelations and breakthroughs."—Micheal Bernard Beckwith.

Practice free self-thinking. Do not judge your thoughts or ideas. Be honest with yourself. Question everything told, read, and heard. Question your reasons for doing something. Through free-thinking, there is awareness of realness. Education is essential to promote a process of thinking with consciousness. There is a five-step process used to engage your mind and spirit in openness:

1. Understand deeply through the acquisition of wisdom (understand the larger picture).
2. Take accountability in your choices of awareness.
3. Raise questions.
4. Follow your flow of ideas and thoughts.
5. Shift today!

Understand

To uncover the ego in our ability to think without conditions of unawareness, understanding these two concepts is vital:

- Logical fallacy is an error in reasoning that renders an argument invalid. Our judgment on personal thought processes is the ego way of disempowering others to express freely.
- Cognitive bias is holding onto one's preferences and beliefs regardless of contrary information. Our conditioning on our views is the ego way of empowering unawareness in the mind and spirit.

Our ability to think without the presence of the ego impacts our application of knowledge. How are you applying learned knowledge in your life? Our immediate steps after gaining knowledge should be to process and use understanding in the best-fitting areas of our lives. Things unfold to reveal what is already there, meaning everything happens under the presented lesson. Do we accept the order of life to recognize our true state?

We should be aware of what is severing the connection with our authentic nature. How in-tune are you with your inner guidance? Why are we taught to learn so much about the world and not enough about ourselves? The emphasis is always on the world around us with no balance of understanding our true nature. There is not enough emphasis on our internal self. When can we return to us? When is that time acceptable? Now.

Accountability

We must emphasize the power of choice and the implications of holding yourself accountable for the choices you make. By keeping yourself responsible for decisions in your life, paths light up from the power of choices. All things happen as intended, whether they're "good" and "bad" (subjective terms). Does love come from understanding? How does that align with the power of choice? How can you be more vulnerable when you understand?

How can you identify a soulmate if you haven't connected with your soul? The soul resides on a spiritual level within yourself. To gain access to this level, it takes self-discovery, self-awareness, and self-realization. We're all interconnected through our souls. We connect with our soulmates (i.e., physically, emotionally, mentally, and most of all, spiritually). But what is a soulmate? A deep spiritual connection to our spiritual being that promotes eternal love and happiness for each other without condition, attachment, or toxic energy. To achieve this, both parties connect spiritually and internally. If both parties do not connect to their spirit, identifying a soulmate is null. You must know your authentic self, first.

Getting to know your soul connection with yourself and others comes in the form of healthy relationships. But what is a healthy relationship? The connection between a person(s) on any level (i.e., physical, mental, emotional, or spiritual) without attachment and acceptance of impermanence. A relationship with attachment is an illusion. It's a scapegoat to deeper personal issues that project on to another person. It's essential to create relationships without attachment by doing the inner work to get closer to your higher being and embrace the unique experience in the present moment. The soul connection to yourself and others in the world around forms the pure feeling of love and connection without the ego.

How does our relationship with the power play into our internal and external connections? For example, our need to control intimacy, personal contact, professional association, work, and money. Our role of power in these relationships rooted in the ego and not the real power of our soul. The ego wants influence in our life, so it tries to show that in our relationships.

The ego will create an attachment to who we have been (i.e., our ego-driven self). We'll find ourselves not reluctant to shifts, fear shifts in our lives, and uncomfortable with transformation. When does it end? Now. The universal concept of attachment to people or things to feel complete has been tough to grasp for many individuals.

From the ego perspective, the idea of wholeness is conditional upon people or things, but we refuse to accept and understand the fact that attachments build mentally and express physically and emotionally. It is possible to get to a state of non-attachment by removing conditional thinking from your world. Our design is to be whole beings and experience life unconditionally.

A relationship built on unconditional care creates longevity and depth in the foundation. The honeymoon stage can be an illusion when intent and false self is present. Reveal our true selves and love ourselves. Encourage care and listen to our authentic being in every encounter. Do you have the awareness to pinpoint qualities you appreciate in your relationships? For me, honesty, trust, loyalty, love, and compassion are always at the forefront of my relationships.

Superficial relationships do not last, and when one or both parties discover that the relationship basis was on external conditions and conditional behavior, which reveals an insecure foundation. The relationship ends at that moment, regardless of the parties' will to stay together. You give up the fruitfulness and desire to extend yourself. Refrain from living in a superficial state and begin to connect more with people and things without identification. Look at someone's character beyond external dimensions of themselves (i.e., material things, careers, wealth, and education degrees). Refrain from living in a superficial state and begin to connect more with people and things without identification.

During and after any relationship, reflection is essential, all intimate relationships with family, friends, partners, and children. The goal is to learn, thrive, and to take advantage of any opportunity for evolution by checking the current state of your relationship with other beings. This time is not a task but, your responsibility to create space for peace and embrace the happy life we want to live with the people most close to us.

A disproportion of inner work will create conflict in relationships as a distortion of growth exists. Each person must put in work. Encourage each other and drive a higher frequency, but you cannot make anyone do the work because it negates true intentions in their own life. As it relates to the relationship, there can be disharmony in the stunted growth of an individual. Be careful not to resonate with the person's frequency, but keep in mind the transcendent of your own. The acknowledgment of your ability to stand alone and do the necessary inner work holds high value in any relationship in your life.

Our internal issues stand tall in our relationships and disguise as relationship issues. There is a tendency to bounce back personal matters in a relationship. The issues intensify because another party involves in our trauma through association. Be able to acknowledge and reflect on your problems, and be mindful not to bring these issues into relationships; we desire to be healthy. It is important to enhance your well-being in a relationship and to focus on your issues while engaging in a relationship with others.

Often, there is a fear of growing due to the drift in a relationship. This fear prevents us from reaching higher levels of personal growth because of the fear of leaving another person behind. The ego shapes this mindset and prevents us from evolution. But true love prepares us in this situation, because we may not evolve or be together at the same stage, we will always love each other and want the best for each other. Unconsciousness is one of the significant causes of personal confusion about relationship drifts.

How can you understand someone, and you're not present in your own life? This question eludes to a contradiction of the phrase, "I am here for you." The focus you bring to your development (i.e., spiritually, mentally, and emotionally) is the energy you put into relationships. When you're not increasing your frequency and capacity to be your best self, your relationships will embody this negligence. The reason you're not attracting people or things right to your spirit is that you're unavailable to your authentic self.

Are you the focus point in your life? Do you consider yourself the star? Or are you an extra playing background to all the others you made stars in your life? It's so easy to lose focus on yourself in life but, remember: this is your life— your movie. We create choices, manifest energy, and execute actions to bring us closer to our authentic being. Any outcome comes from the choices we make and the Divine. The universe will give whatever you're worthy to receive.

What are you doing to manifest your reality? What type

of energy are you putting out in the universe? Considering the present moment, think about how your truth and power plays a part in the world. We construct our images of what we want, who we are, where we want to be, when to be who we truly are, why we emit specific energy, and how we can shift. Often, we neglect answering these self-questions with honesty driven from our authentic beliefs.

Happiness should be unconditional; it derives from true unconditional love. But does this concept of happiness comes with spiritual maturity? We make choices to love unconditional or conditional. Our unconditional love is the pure state of love that is free of any derivatives of fear. So, our conditional love is full of fear as its synonymous with the ego. The ego places conditions to keep us from loving freely and without reservations.

Society has made ways for us to be present without knowing and take our minds away from reality; for example, entertainment, media, and sports. But why does it seem impossible for us to be present in our own lives and vested in personal growth and development? Is it because we don't know how to? Is it because we rather ignore it? Is it because we are content with our reality? Or are we afraid? Yes, that's it, we're fearful of actually looking inward and discovering our actual being. We learn concepts of fear (i.e., all the ideas attached to fear), sometimes not enough emphasis on love.

Question

Most times, people don't ask in-depth questions about their life because they don't want to shift their perspective. Their fear becomes prevalent. They become content with the unknown and resistance to closeness with self. There is a disregard for any self-reflection.

With inner awareness through reflection, we'll understand how much we were in states of denial. This denial prevented us from accepting "it is, what it is." This notion can be hard to take because we run from the truth most times to keep our ego alive. But the sooner we acknowledge the fact; our liberation will begin.

The deliverance continues in our acknowledgment of strengths and areas of improvement. Have you ever created a list of your strengths and talents? Try completing that list then focus on your top three. Visualize how these strengths can serve the greater good of your community and the world. How can you help your presence and others with these recognized strengths?

Let's talk about our areas of improvement. These hidden gems are for growth. Areas that will speed up our growth as beings if we discover, accept, and use them to service our awareness of evolution. Create a list of your improvement areas and highlight your top three. Continue to find ways to work on your areas to resist the ego and expel its hold on your ability to conquer by living a fruitful life free from fear.

Some of our strengths and areas of improvement can be a part of our conditioning. The environments we grew up in can be an embodiment of these traits around us fed to our subconscious mind. So, consider this after identifying your strengths and improvement areas.

Your areas of improvement can be present through someone's strengths. You'll find yourself being resentful and uncomfortable around that person. Instead of acknowledging why you're feeling that way or what is triggering the feelings, this feeling could be an opening for growth. Our improvement areas have untapped power. We are capable of doing any and everything we put our minds. So next time you find yourself triggered by someone's strengths, take a look at yourself, and kindle a flame of courage to reach your full potential.

Your limits are boundless—in the theory of mathematics, any limit function of x approaching zero does not exist. As this is a practical example, we can apply this example in our life.

A concrete example is limiting yourself or potential based on external limits by others. Never give up your right to liberty as it will take a toll on your soul through mental and spiritual enslavement.

Potential means you have the power to be your best self, just not in this present moment. Shouldn't we intend to be our best self in every moment? How and when did a term that is so subjective become standard? Why are we stuck on potential and ignore the reality of things? For example, we always claim that someone or something has potential without accepting who or what is present to us. We pass judgment based on our perception. But this judgment has ties to the ego and not our authentic self. Your true conscious self does not judge; your unconscious self judges your being and everyone else.

People will reveal themselves to you if you ask the right questions. I'm talking about full-body questions that go deeper than the surface level. People tend to put on a facade when you first meet; it's up to you to get to know that person and allow them to reveal the true self.

How big is true self-love in our society? Do superficial actions mask it? Do people know what real self-love is? Are we intentional with the attention and respect we give to ourselves? Can we make a shift today and stand by our authentic being full of consciousness? Let's escape any preconceived notions of self-love and internally define this concept meaning to our soul. Our self-love is the creed for our soul. The more profound appreciation for all that we are and conscious living brings forth our true self.

Are you subscribing to the popular image by saying you're working on your inner self, or are you practicing conscious living? This idea of false representation is a state of unconsciousness, and inflation of the ego, the external perception of being favorable to the unconscious. An intimate understanding of being is helpful to the conscious, which identify ego and insecurities. Refrain from creating false love or an illusion through the ego.

Flow

What is your flow of life? What are your contributions to the universe? For me, I inspire through passion and ambition (or IPA—inspire, passion, and ambition). My flow is intentional. I'm not flowing through dead-end streams. My flow is targeting vast streams full of purpose in my life. How are you enforcing intentionality in your life?

Can you be present for yourself? Be the right person for yourself and your well-being. The task of being present is simple, create awareness, and be proactive in every moment —the ability to be your best self in every way you can to bring forth your authentic presence.

Your authentic presence sets actual needs and wants for higher flow. You don't need S-E-X, you need S-C-D (i.e., Self-Care Day). A full day to center yourself, clear your mind, relax, and do things that add value to your well-being. Take the time to think about you! This time includes self-care and balance throughout your life. For me, this means Self-Care Sunday or SCS. My day, I dedicate myself to endowing my spirit holistically (i.e., physically, emotionally, mentally, spiritually, financially, etc.). This day is in conjunction with my daily self-care practices; while I commit to one full day of self-care, it doesn't take away every day focus on self-care. There is no such thing as focusing too much on your well-being when it provides a radiant presence in the universe.

But how does SCD look? This practice is different for everyone due to their personal needs. Though, I have a holistic approach to SCD:

- Mentally—awakening with gratitude, meditation, prayer, reading, streaming Sunday service, and journal to reflect on the thoughts of the moment.
- Physically—stretching, engaging in yoga, pampering my body (i.e., paying attention to my face, hands, and feet), eating hearty meals, preparing meals for the week, and soaking my body in a bath to reduce any tension and increase relaxation.
- Spiritually—encouraging positive emotions, thoughts, and space for my true being. Placing my spiritual self in the universe and invoking stillness at the moment.
- Financially—reviewing my finances and observing my spending habits. Consciously prepare for financial transactions for the upcoming week.
- Emotionally—positive self-talk, aromatherapy, soothing music, sound therapy, and proper rest are essential for me.

There is no particular order to fulfill these needs. Still, I limit distractions to achieve a joyful experience. I refrain from social interactions unless they are necessary, as this is my day for quality time. I'm rarely on the phone or texting, but I use social media platforms as a way to share my experience (i.e., to post, respond, and exit the platform). To provide an example of what is a day full of self-care. To inspire and promote healing of self by engaging in similar experiences. Grounded ideas of fulfillment can uplift your health, clear mind, improved memory, better sleep, more energy, lack of anxiety, lack of depression, and quality breathing.

Let's zoom in on one of my mind practices. Through journaling, your physical self becomes a third party to your thoughts and words written on the page. This space is a judgment-free zone with the mission to unpack any disparities to get to your authentic being. Journaling brings me so much joy and peace. I journal daily to maintain a peace of mind and to fulfill my desire for enlightenment. I always keep my journal near!

My spiritual self manifests through literature, podcasts, journaling, and listening to my real thoughts about the universe. Three things developed: affirmation, inspiration, and introspection through self-evaluating questions and honest responses. Imagine having all the world spiritual leaders easily accessible. We do! While we may not have direct contact, we do have indirect contact (i.e., literature, podcast, videos, etc.). Knowledge sharing is available across literature and the internet to hold words of wisdom flowing from spiritual leaders in the universe.

Guard your own time! Make the time to take care of you! Always express and show appreciation for your mind, body, and soul. Are you connecting with your presence? If not, you're creating separation between the present moment and your authentic self, which should be one. Inwardly, decide at which level you would like to dwell spiritually. Think about your state of mind in this present moment and how you hope to connect. Some daily spiritual practices that I use are:

- Give gratitude to at least one thing in the morning
- Restrict any phone activity when I wake up for at least 30 minutes
- Listen to gospel music and podcasts
- Read and write in my journal
- Meditate, deep breathing exercises, working out, yoga, and solitude when necessary

The daily practice of gratitude is the jumpstart of a joyful day. Do you have a gratitude list or mental note of things you're most grateful for? For me, life, my presence, my mind, my family/support system, my awareness, and this moment are some things I have on my gratitude list. Never compromise your happiness, and always protect your peace. Always operate in a place of love and gratitude!

Creativity plays a role in your flow, and appreciation for the creative part of your mind is fundamental. What are some prominent places where your mind flourishes in creativity? My artistic mind thrives by or in water, in my home, and during the night. Taking a shower or bath helps clear my mind and spark creativity. Watching the waves of the sea or watching the water flow deepens my creative power. During the night, there is a flow state of artistic practice that allows me to be attentive to my creative nature. The comfortability and vibrant frequency of my home bring forth creative action, words, and thoughts. Creativity guides visualization in your life.

The value in visualizing how to achieve goals, overcome

situations, and live a happy life is precious. Goal setting is excellent but, envisioning a plan of action to fulfill goals is exceptional. Commit to seeing yourself achieve your purpose before engaging in the execution—examples of visualizing goals, vision boarding, or creating your mental vision of attainment. Conflict resolution can be difficult without effective communication.

Most situations arise from ineffective communication. Study the art of conversation and practice in your everyday life. Living a happy life is all in the attitude you have about life and mental capacity for the shift to your authentic self. There is much power in our authentic being, which carries over in our perception of reality. Our evolution from an egoic state of mind will get us closer to the path of eternal happiness.

How can you support yourself at any moment and activate your authentic inner power? Self-realizing when you need to draw that power and release at any moment. There will be challenges, but you're powerful beyond imagination with the ability to overcome any obstacle. How are you using your power to help the world?

Motivation is integral in the universe. Who motivates you? To be honest, the answer to this question took me some time to express and accept my response. I've always been self-motivated. My motivation to lead by example, moving in alignment, and being the person; I want to be was still my authentic intentions. To be honest, it took me time to accept this as I felt pure self-appraisal and self-motivation were uncommon.

When you think of who motivates you, it's rarely yourself; it's frequently an external being. So society uses the idea of self-motivation as an adjective in situations without the true nature of the context. Consider that motivation and inspiration are not the same. There is always a capacity to create inspiration by the characteristics of others, but the root of your drive will be different. As my real motivator, I'm continually giving myself feedback on my intentions, goals, and vision of life. These self-checks keep me aware and open to the evolution of being.

How can you motivate people to connect spiritually? Be the display of a shift in behavior in your life. People will notice the practice of spirituality, which provides a reason for the release of unconsciousness through learned actions.

Idea

From childhood to adulthood, we unconsciously carry over trauma by not facing matters. We have imprints from our childhood that carried over into adulthood. Their marks revealed in our identity, relationships, and perception of the world. For years, we prescribe suffering without knowing until we wake up and realize that our early demise was conditioning.

Now, is the time to stop your unconscious acts and deal with the root of your problems, yourself. Acknowledge the emotions and thoughts you felt at past times is essential to our forward progress. To get over traumas, you have to go beyond the surface level into your soul. Dwelling on the surface level does not promote healing. Always go to the root of your emotions.

Family members can be triggers to trauma. We may still feel uneasy about past situations. Simultaneously, they can be barriers for us to overcome the issue. So, in a way, we allow them to absorb our power and prevent our growth. Firsthand, I have learned that no one should take away your strength and your ability to evolve. Our family members can keep us in a traumatic mindset as we may not accept the facts of reality. It's time for you to reclaim your power and be accountable in our own life. No longer allow people or things to impede on your journey of evolution. By consciously removing conditions from your mind, triggers will no longer have control over your growth. We can no longer play the victim of our circumstances. The time is now to move forward.

What is your perception of time? What is your understanding of shifts? How can both be impactful in your life? Now let's review some ways to apply your responses to your childhood.

How to look back into your childhood? Start with your inner self:

1. Identify moments of trauma.
2. Acknowledge your emotions at that moment.
3. Be accountable for your role in decision making.
4. Surrender to that moment and leave in the past.
5. Be present for introspection.
6. Begin healing.
7. Move forward.

I can stand here today and say confidently; the odds were in my favor, growing up. I've had many experiences the universe would deem traumatic. I see all I have experienced as learning experiences that have transformed into growth opportunities. They were just experiences at the moment. These moments did not define me because I did not allow myself to identify with them, but they gave me the ability to understand and embody my true self. Self-determination and motivation kept me moving forward.

Emotional thinking focuses on your false self, and you

hold on to old emotions, as it reinforces your identity and creates a narrative. I'm sure you heard these phrases before: "My experiences made me who I am today" or "The hurt I experienced in my past is why I'm who I am today." You are free from experiences unless you identify with them.

Do you believe everything in your life you've created? Partially, this is true. Everything that involves your power of choice creates your reality but, most often, parents or guardians take our power of choice away as a child. Once that absence of choice is evident, we unconsciously believe we don't have the power of choice as we grow into adulthood. We must be aware of the power of choice in our life to increase our mindfulness. Always do what is best for you; you're the creator!

Shift

Structuring your mind is when you learn 1+1=2; this learned behavior made sense in the theory of mathematics. This lesson instilled within us from repetition and logic. As we restructure our minds without conditions to foster awareness, peace, and unconditional love, we must keep in mind that this is a learned behavior that was not always available to us like mathematics. There may not be many practitioners of these themes in our lives, so make efforts to seek guidance and understanding. How do we explore this particular knowledge? All this knowledge needs special attention and practice to come full turn as a holistic lifestyle.

For consciousness, we have access to many spiritual leaders whose purpose is to heal and inspire others on platforms like the internet and through literature. We have easy access to podcasts, books, interviews, and studies of people sharing fantastic awareness content. We must extrapolate this information and reflect on our personal lives, especially when we don't have direct access to these practitioners. For peace, we examine our mental capacity and environments to see if they align with the ideals of peace. An unclear mind can extend your suffering and continue egoic thoughts. Our environments play a huge part as well; the surrounding people can evoke peace and growth or disruption and stagnation. So, we must make choices to stay put in specific environments or move on for evolution. Clarity and positive energy go hand in hand!

For unconditional love, we must revisit our roots, family, and self. Our family dynamic reveals how the expression of shared love in the household, which plays a role in our nature to place conditions or not in love. We don't know how affected we are until we become older, and issues surface in relationships with other beings. The recognition of self-love imprint growing up, and significance, as you grow older is essential. It's powerful once you realize how much self-love radiates high frequencies of emotions in every encounter. Self-love mirrored on real values and deep internal understanding without external factors. Internal and external exploration of knowledge strengthens the unconditional reconstruction of reality.

Through my journey of enlightenment, I've affirmed that breaking generational curses is more about healing than achievements and creating wealth; the generational curses of developed qualities from past traumas passed down, and all the ideas of unconsciousness, conditioned behavior, and thinking. We must make it our priority to lift the curse and radiate higher awareness. Going forward, let's make efforts and hold ourselves accountable to put an end to these curses.

Be open to transformative thinking. Get to the foundation of who you are and your purpose in the universe. There is always space for advancement in our being. Our minds are powerful, but we must explore ways of using it in a valuable way. Rid it from conditional thinking, discover the depth, and expand our questions for further understanding of life. Be your responsible partner in seeking knowledge for your well-being and fulfill your real vision. By way of transformative thinking, we can share our best self to the universe.

Thinking outside the box is essential to a transformative lifestyle. We challenge traditional views by re-defining words with assigned meaning and assessing the implications in your life with openness. Not to identify with conditional thinking and to open your mind to the endless possibilities of the universe, you've to go beyond being in the box and expand our horizon through awareness. We can no longer be a victim of unconsciousness. Our beingness is limitless, as you no longer experience a non-transformative lifestyle that keeps you captive to unconsciousness.

There is always talk about different worlds. I recognize two worlds exist in the universe: your world and the world of humanity. One is personal, and the other is interpersonal. We connect with our authentic selves and others in this universe. We create our world, and the world of humanity creates through the totality of our existence. Both are real, depending on your state of awareness. It can be challenging to understand the concept of these worlds as we were condition to believe there was only one world. In turn, we identified only with the world of humanity disregarding the world of self and soul counterparts. The universe encompasses different worlds beyond the two I've recognized as being prominent. There is an interconnection of these worlds, creating one universe.

This statement is not scientifically sound but a way to infuse the theme of thought. Imagine a yellow tree grown next to a body of blue water. Based on our fundamental understanding of colors, what reveals when you look at the water? What does this mean to you? I want you to think about this visually, mentally, and spiritually. There is no right or wrong answer. My response is in the reflection part of this chapter.

Reflect

1. What labels do you create for yourself? Why do you create these labels? Do they provide a sense of identity? How can you get closer to your authentic being without labels?
2. What makes you unique?
3. Write down some questions you would like to ask your inner being. Try to respond to these questions honestly and without judgment of feelings/ thoughts from the ego.
4. Complete the sentence: I would like the universe to know that I...
5. Today teach something you've recently learned that can benefit another being.
6. How would you describe your effort in establishing fruitful relationships in your life?

Prompt response:

In my eyes, a green tree. The reflection of the yellow tree in the blue body of water creates a green tree reflected in the water. The yellow tree becomes an afterthought. The yellow tree is an external representation of the phrase: it's more than meets the eye. The exterior is not always the same as the interior and clears from a conscious perspective. The blue body of water becomes a lens to see something special. The blue body of water is an internal representation of the phrase: show me who you are, and I'll tell you who you are. Through acceptance and conscious understanding, nothing can hide. This outlook doesn't exist without considering introspection and extrospection. Our reflections of things provoke the thought of new revelations and meanings in our world. Our preexisting beliefs shift due to understanding and openness. Scientifically, there is no change in color; the tree remains yellow. But, now something we perceive separately has a connection that promotes the idea of unity. The tree and body of water are one, not different, but connected in the universe.

7

TRUTH

"You always know the answer when you're willing to listen to your truth."—Oprah Winfrey.

There is nothing off-limits when you seek the truth about your authentic self—not even moving away from your unconscious mind. The conditioned thinking and domestication we have developed over time have put us in an unconscious state. The state of unawareness has imposed obstacles in our consciousness. The true self has a mask. As you expand your awareness, you begin to see the truth of things in the universe—promoting a shift in perspective that opens your eyes to the false self. We begin to see people and things for who and what they are at the moment. Our universe reveals the truth of beingness without pretenses we create for ourselves.

The ultimate truth of beingness is that we are all created by love. This love has different forms: love from the Divine, our higher power, love from guardians/ parents, spoken or unspoken. Our capacity for love is enough, so why is it so difficult to love? Is it our unwillingness? Our past traumas? Or is it the ego? The challenge lies in our fear. The light we have inside our soul has untapped potential to alleviate us from the darkness produced by fear. The sooner we draw from this light and live in love, we'll be closer to internal liberation.

Is your soul close to liberation?

Imagine being stuck in a cornfield, and you're trying to find a way through. There is no sense of urgency, and you're content with in the field but, know there is fulfillment when you get out. You meet your authentic self—you are now one, one with yourself in consciousness. This scenario represents our battle in an unconscious world where we become complacent and not push ourselves to get to know who we are. But, finally feeling free the day we take strides to realize our authentic self. We must be aware of our intentions and don't confine ourselves to the unknown. In your life, plan to be present to create clarity of purpose and understanding.

The matching of actions and intentions creates alignment. Misalignment reveals a contradiction with actions and intentions displaying dishonesty with yourself. Misrepresented intentions put up a temporary smokescreen of our authentic self. Let's stand clear of any smokescreens and move authentically through life. Be a representation of your true intentions: interactions with people, engagement at places, and values in the universe. I believe goalsetting is a form of setting your intentions. In this form, it's essential to create a plan of action, acknowledge your effort, and observe results. Our clear intentions bring mindfulness to efforts and achievements while remaining accountable.

Be in harmony with intention and manifest peace. Are you creating peace in life?

Create

To begin the creation of peace, release the ego from this moment. There is no room for unconsciousness in your mind. Our ability to come into our spiritual being through the truth will set our soul free; our willingness to surrender fully without resistance to the present moment. Don't stand in the way of the plans of the Divine—things happen for a reason. Life plans out the way it's supposed to, and we must be willing to observe our higher power.

Be honest, are you ready to be present for you? Respond honestly and begin your awakening. Now ask, are you available for presence? Are you willing to surrender your unconscious self to consciousness and eternal happiness? The most significant moment in life is when you're ready to become closer to your authentic self.

There is nothing that can defeat you; the Divine flows through you with great power. My higher power can never be second when I put myself first—the Divine in me. When I pray, I don't pray to an external being; I pray to an inner being. The Divine is inside of me, I'm part of a higher power, and my connection to my higher self is where it resides. When I refer to the Divine, in essence, I'm referring to my higher self and any other being with a connection to their higher self as we're interconnected.

You have everything you need. Your identification with external extensions is not necessary to live full.

Live in a world where you accommodate your real needs and wants. Are you addressing your actual needs (i.e., needs of your soul)? How are you distinguishing between what your soul needs and wants? Make a conscious effort to understand the depths of yourself to recognize what you need in life without identification.

Is identification making you resistant toward growth? What is preventing you from achieving your highest self at this moment? Be mindful when you're holding yourself back from greatness. You cannot become what you are already—greatness. You are returning to the state in which originate your greatness, so don't resist growth.

What can you build to outlast the ego? Unconditional love, peace, harmony, and bravery to move away from the ego. The ego tries to prevent us from greatness and longevity with our authentic beings, which is the spiritual union our ego attempts to deprive us of daily. Enlightenment instills love instead of fear, severing our attachment with fear through love, and using the soul wisdom.

You are the only person who can promote a shift in your life.

Consistency brings habit, and a habit becomes a lifestyle. Self-discipline is essential in forwarding progress! The Divine prepares us for forwarding progress, as this is imperative to the liberation of the soul. We can do more than one thing; our capacity for greatness is limitless. Permit yourself a lifestyle without limits to your authentic being.

Focus on doing better at this moment instead of focusing on what you do incorrectly, as this gets us out of a limited mind. We add too much emphasis to the past and not enough attention to the present. Working from a place of presence brings out an opportunity for advancement in our own life. I'm always looking at ways to improve my being! I work every day to practice what I preach—not allowing anything to get in the way of my eternal peace and happiness. The fruitfulness of life is more apparent through this practice.

Be the pupil in your school of evolution and committed to your spiritual work. This school of evolution is not for change but, shift to the true self. In reality, you no longer allow the ego to blind you but, have a clear vision of your authentic self.

Reality

Often the reality of things is challenging to talk about; it's easier not to face reality and remain dazed. I encourage you to take things for what they are, face reality! Even if it's uncomfortable and goes against everything, you believe— there is less suffering in the truth. In the beginning, the fact may hurt, but it will set you free! Consciously create space in your life for the truth!

There is a distinction between what is real and what you believe to be true. The difference lies in our mental perception of reality. Often, we create illusions in our minds to fit what we want to be real. These illusions prevent the clarity and soundness of the soul as we become the victim of the ego through self-created deception. We know the truth but allowed the ego to make an unconscious choice not to believe over our intuition. The concept of spiritual discernment becomes significant in our daily life as it is the ability to distinguish what is real and what is false. Be affirmative with your decisions as it relates to your truth of intuition.

You shift perspective by believing and accepting the truth; be honest and refrain from feeling like you can change or make someone do something. We are responsible for ourselves.

It is not your responsibility to fix someone else. Often, we confuse our love with someone and responsibility for their care, which is not on us. Your primary concern is to rebuild yourself and promote wellness in your own life. I've affirmed that love is more internal than external. The root of love is internal, and the expression of love is external. Love is not superficial. Your real power is in spirit. But your spiritual responsibility is to connect with other souls and tap into the divinity of the universe.

In reality, unconscious decisions and the absorption of responsibility form regret. Throughout my life, assertiveness warded off any feelings of regret. I've never regretted any decision as it stemmed from my choice. My decisive attitude in any decision mirrored my values then. I encourage you always to have your best interest at heart first:

- Never compromise your values.
- Never compromise your morals.
- Never compromise your happiness.

I've always done the best I can to showcase my best self, and now there is a means to celebrate coming into my authentic self. I'm appreciative of the growth that allowed me to get to this point of spiritual restoration. I'm no longer captive to the egoic way of solitude. I'm awakening to the actual being I've always been. At this point, there is no room for regression.

I'm no longer falling victim to matching energy. I'm setting the tone and enthusiasm I will receive. The energy presented in my environment may not be authentic to my frequency. I'm no longer giving people that much power over my presence. The impact of unconsciousness will not impact my level of consciousness. You should always be your true self despite the circumstance. Never allow any condition to deviate from who you are. I ask myself this in environments with low-frequency energy: what matters most to me right now? My happiness and peace matter most. It has been my lifestyle to continue the practice of consciousness and intent. I feel free! A bad day shouldn't have to exist when you're the creator of your reality and energy frequency.

Find the strength to be the authority in your life. Be influential, comfortable, self-assured, and shield yourself from any moments of fear.

Repeat these words:
I'm authentically me; it's impossible to be anyone else!

Do you believe in yourself? Respond honestly. Allow your soul to speak as you uncover any certainty or uncertainty. There is strength in being vulnerable. The expelling of the ego showcases the power in being open with your true feelings and thoughts. We should no longer be captive to our emotions and non-expression. Our design of the truth is we should be expressive as spiritual beings, and to assure that our soul energy expression brings forth a different life experience.

A great French philosopher, Pierre Teilhard de Chardin, said: we are not human beings having a spiritual experience; we are spiritual people having a human experience. At this moment, how would you describe your soul's energy? Is your soul emitting positivity through awareness or negativity through unawareness?

At this moment, how would you describe your karma? Have you treated people and the universe with love and compassion? Karmic energy will reciprocate what you put out in the world. Be mindful of the type of energy you radiate.

Your soul is forever. Be alive to karma in your awakening.

Presence

What does awakening mean to you? To me, it's heightened awareness through integration with your authentic self and higher power. This awakening is prompt by a shift in perspective from mental and spiritual alignment. You're already complete as you are, conscious effort to become closer to our authentic being is needed. Wholeness requires ongoing work! A life not fragmented between ego-self and authentic self. This complete life requires regular self-checking to keep channeling of authentic power going.

I'm no longer operating from a place of incomplete thought without regard to awareness and wisdom. I'm moving into a home of complete thinking with education and outreach. I can no longer be captive to ignorance with guiding concepts of liberation and prosperity. Be the fullness that you are right where you're at, don't misguide yourself into misery over things you have no control over. Be the shift you want in your life! Shift your legacy!

My parents created me out of love regardless of their past traumas (both individual and joint). I believe children are blessings. Children bring the lessons of conditional thinking and domestication into perspective. It is the Divine's way of bringing holistic teachings from birth to adulthood. Guardians and parents unconsciously reconcile past traumas and inject into children, and sadly, pain can find a way to the present and prevent children from being conscious. Most of society is not taught self-awareness and fostered in the household.

Consideration of alternative teachings when raising children may have an impact on the universe. Explore consciousness, compassion, mindfulness, and unconditional love as children grow up. As these are themes not emphasize enough in our lives, we cannot allow our deficiency play a part in a child's life. Begin to seek wisdom and practice application to be more present.

In the early ages of childhood, there is a void in promotion void of freethinking; conditioned thinking is in the center. Children learn to think a certain way, and when they get older, the expectation is freethinking to make decisions. How does that make sense? It doesn't. Awareness and proactive teachings bring an understanding of self.

What are some qualities you want children to learn from you? For me, consciousness, mindfulness, dedication, compassion, empathy, ambition, and open-mindedness.

Suffering passes from generation to generation by not practicing mindfulness, so now we must begin to create understanding and love. Ultimately, to prevent future generations from this cycle of suffrage.

Consciousness is not a concept that children cannot understand; it's a concept that's not fostered and taught enough. There is a need for higher knowledge and well deserved for our future. We all can use our creativity in an empowering way to assist in passing down wisdom. Raising more conscious beings involves three primary shifts: paying attention to your inner being, to their state of awareness, and accepting the present moment.

Self-passion goes a long way in well-being for our world and the universe.

Passion

Have you ever created a list of your true desires? Try forming a list without tangible things. Refrain from allowing time to dictate your actions instead use this moment to express your true desires. Let go of your egoic idea of time and execution. This list can be a conscious reminder of your passion. What is your soul telling you that you deserve? Will you honor your desires?

What is your vision of a successful life? My idea of a successful life is to be eternally happy and to have peace in being. Also, to fulfill my life purpose to inspire healing in others. I've made this a reality by continuing my self-work, moving with consciousness, compassion, love, and putting myself first while being able to uplift others. I'm ridding myself of past perspectives and being open to new perspectives, moving with intention every day to shape my life of divinity. Now, what type of characteristics do you need to embody to be your definition of success? Consider these characteristics in your vision of a successful life. Be present to what it takes to be your concept of a successful individual in the universe.

We must speak our success into existence and negate negative thoughts of failure.

If something is important to you, start now! Not tomorrow or next year. Begin the manifestation of energy needed to do what you set out to do. The top excuse is: I'm going to start tomorrow or next year. When does the cycle of inactivity end? When do we hold ourselves accountable in the present moment? The more we push things back, the longer our full potential is not tapped into our lives feel incomplete. For example, I consistently set new goals each day, but through my progress and assessment, I hold myself accountable. I use my birthday and New Year's as a starting point for the progress of new goals I set for myself. These are moments of reflection and intentional shifts to transcend a higher presence in the universe. This state includes letting things go that don't serve my authentic being and goal setting to be accountable for conscious shifts. These are starting points for measurement not, always starting point for new intention. There is a difference. Goals are continuous tasks with the practice of intention with your values. Most importantly, I set goals but allow myself to be present in every moment.

Love and Kind

Consciousness is yours! The Divine sets knowledge as the will for all beings.

The Divine also prepares a will for happiness—the soul commandment for peace. We can achieve this will of happiness by introspection (i.e., looking at our internal environment) and extrospection (i.e., looking at our external environment). We must look within ourselves and beyond ourselves (i.e., non-self). To reflect and gain a better understanding of our authentic being and our intended contribution to the world- our purpose. This purpose is neither big nor small but significant to our soul's duty. When we think of purpose, our minds prescribe to a grand idea instead of taking in the spiritual meaning of purpose. We need to observe the production of energy in introspection and extrospection for a prosperous life through wisdom and happiness.

In retrospect, spiritual principles would seep out of me, but I wasn't fully ready to listen. I was always self-assured but wasn't aware of the true intentions of the soul. Now I know that the truth and soulful messages were always present; I needed to awaken to the attainability of my authentic power, fully. Often, we overlook messages from our authentic selves, as we may not be ready to receive. Through reflection, you can recognize how your intuition has given wisdom to your mind and guided your decisions.

Our spiritual being is always present in our lives, but we must regain closeness needed to refresh our relationship. Never miss out on opportunities to learn about yourself.

Our highest order is to give to humanity. But the only way to give without conditions is by providing to ourselves, unconditionally. Build a foundation that involves compassion, happiness, joy, love, and wellness. When we offer with conditions, we do not meet our highest order as its clouded by the ego. Faithful giving comes without condition and aligns with the soul. We cannot give what is not accessible in our lives at the moment but come from a place of attainability and add to others as we add to ourselves. We must continuously add value to our lives and be willing to add value to another's life. We can no longer be selfish but selfless to act with love, which is evident through our self-love.

Self-love is the root of loving others. The way you show love to others is the way you show love to yourself. If you lack self-love, this will show in all your relationships past and present. If you're full of self-love, love and happiness will be prevalent in your life.

Repeat this:
I am loved. I am me. I am purposeful.

Love the deepest parts of your inner being. Love yourself from inside out in every moment. Show appreciation for all that you are. Our true depths are like hidden gems of our nature. We must rediscover these gems and apply the pressure of their value in our life. We are remarkable beings with infinite possibilities and power.

Compassion and empathy coexist. The only way forward

is the well-being of others. Our kindness helps us to understand, and empathy generates feelings for others.

Empathic abilities evolve through heightened spiritual presence. As a person with empathic intelligence, I've seen my abilities grow by connecting more spiritually to myself. I always had an empathic nature to my being that allowed me to understand other emotions without full disclosure of information. But, unconsciously, I would find myself absorbing other emotions that were not as healthy as they distorted my emotions at times. I learned to be present with compassion and open to empathy without the absorption of feelings. The empathy you share can be the support needed for others to get through situations.

You've got the power to forgive and release! There is no reason to mentally dwell in a situation that compromises your happiness and peace. Be intentional with yourself and be proactive in your life. Allow yourself to move forward, heal, and permit conscious living. Everything in life happens for a reason! Let all things that don't empower your higher being go! I'll affirm, you'll feel lighter, free, peaceful, and graceful by honoring your discipline.

What is your code of honor? I have a few disciplines of honor that I'm living through: tell nothing but the truth; be honest with yourself, be honest with others; whatever you put your mind to, you'll achieve. You need to set boundaries as it relates to your code of honor. Be careful not to allow anyone to disregard your limits through respect. The connection to your code of honor may not resonate with others, and this is perfectly fine.

Connect

There is judgment towards people for shifting when it's the way of the Divine. There is a need to be adaptable to evolution and encourage growth in other's presence. It may be uncomfortable to get to know someone again in their rediscovered state of presence. Their shift in persona can cause intimidation to your prior understanding of a person. To feel comfortable, you'll continuously zone in on the past and not able to be present. The presentation of the current being in front of you goes unnoticed due to personal comfort level.

Mindfulness is meaningful when a person is going through shifts in their life and open ourselves to their shift toward awareness. There may be feelings of possible drifts in the relationship or lack of commonality. This feeling is far from the truth through your practice of mindfulness; acknowledge that the person is living in states of awareness with personal boundaries to unconsciousness. If you're willing to respect certain boundaries and operate in areas where you both live and prosper, the relationship will blossom beyond your imagination.

Through growth, be comfortable introducing or reintroducing yourself to people in your life. You are reviving yourself every day through growth. The person you were yesterday no longer exists because of the knowledge and experience you have acquired today. Never be afraid to let someone know who you are at this moment, which may include sharing your true self. Be your authentic self—set your soul free from restrictions created from unawareness.

In society, there is no real struggle with theory or concepts, but battle with application and practice in life. The conflict comes from our resistance to apply the idea in our life. The struggle is self-created through resistance to growth. To be willing to shift your beliefs every day without resistance or hesitation, you need to be free from conditioning.

Do you accept any accountability in your conditioning? I will be the first to take some responsibility in my conditioning through my ignorance. Mind shifting has abundant wisdom that I was not ready and willing to seek in the world. I allowed for cyclical cycles to continue without boundaries.

For me, it was vital to understand past conditioning no longer serve me, as I seek wisdom, and set boundaries in my life for healing. There is no one to blame for our conditioning, as this was a continuous cycle of ignorance. We must all take accountability to some degree of our conditioning as we allowed it to go on so long without beginning the healing process. Real generational curses stop through awareness and healing to end the cycle of the ego.

Without boundaries, we connect to a process of non-healing. Setting boundaries is like giving the cheat codes to your limits and requesting understanding. It's essential to know your trauma/triggers to set appropriate boundaries for your healing process. Boundaries are universal and should apply to all situations you deem fit.

Be intentional in setting boundaries for yourself and your healing. Be sincere to yourself and safeguard your being:

- As a relates to relationships, communicate, and request respect for your limits. If there is a disregard to your limits, choose how to proceed based on your capacity for the opposition and personal values.
- As it relates to self, be honest, and listen to your authentic being. Respect your values and put

your well-being at the highest priority for
healing. In the case of your noncompliance,
remind yourself of your healing process and the
importance of self-commitments.

Often, your self-boundaries pass-through relationship
boundaries and align with your intentions. Love and respect
should show up in any capacity of your life. There should
never be a reason to pick between the two, as both are integral in the universe.

Universe

Many great individuals in history have come to the realization of evolution and our need for spirituality and
oneness. One that comes to mind quickly is Abraham
Maslow, an American psychologist, who revised his initial
theory of human needs (known as Maslow's hierarchy of
needs). This revision incorporated the idea of self-transcen-
dence, which encompasses the spiritual awakening, free
from the ego, and the unity of being.

The idea goes beyond self and embraces the universe as
a whole. This amendment refers to the evolution of people
and the holistic view of human experience. Our true happiness drives love, not only self-love but love for all. When you
live a life beyond you, you transcend. Our higher power is
infinite!

How are you exposing yourself to the universe? Uncover
the many things the world has to offer and to be mindful of
the great benefits of experience.

Govern your life; you're the ruler:

- Your body is your temple.

- Your mind is your structure of governing.
- Your spirit provides checks and balances by your authentic self.
- Your space is your atmosphere.
- Your relationships are the people you choose in your life.
- Your universe is all other areas around you inspired by love and compassion.

This way of life gives that the ego has no power, yet you can quickly identify it if present in yourself or the universe. To go beyond yourself—you must know yourself! Discover all that you are, and watch yourself continuously! Go beyond the false!

What effort are you pursuing to enforce the oneness of your soul with the universe? Are you able to see the light in your beingness and the world? We don't learn lessons to bring our being to wholeness. These lessons are fundamental to our complete being. Our awareness enables us to see experiences as a means to an end and identify feelings of incompleteness. We are never whole until we can acknowledge our presence in the universe. This presence means consciousness.

Spiritual realization is the fullness of one's authentic self. There is a shift in aligning your true self with reality and the sense of self-empowerment in the universe. This realization is a state every being can access. The insightfulness from our true self deepens our existence. Spiritual realization looks like an inner awakening that brings us whole. There is no more self-separation. My conceptual understanding reveals that we have no permanent identity, as we're ever-changing beings. We must refrain from identifying with personalities and externalities. Our removal of identification creates impermanence by nature. The ego clings to identity as a place to live and thrive. It is simple to attach yourself to a character as a safe place or illusion of more deep-rooted fear. Free yourself from fear and unconsciousness.

Realize your light in the universe!

Reflect

1. Think about your reactions to the truth (i.e., demeanor, responses, etc.). How are you positioning your readiness for the truth? Will you be reluctant or open to the truth?
2. Write a love letter to yourself. Capture the appreciation you have for yourself in this present moment.
3. Write a message that you feel everyone in the universe needs to hear.
4. Complete the sentence: daily words I plan to live by are...
5. How would you define success?
6. What is your current plan for achieving your goals? How can you reconstruct your plan to fit your definition of success? How can your definition of success and new plan help accomplish any goal you set for yourself?
7. What have you learned about yourself?
8. Close your eyes. Create a visual picture of peace and prosperity in your life.

CLOSING

"You experience your soul each time you sense yourself as more than a mind and body, your life as meaningful, or you feel that you have gifts to give and you long to give them."—Gary Zukav.

My learning goals are forever! There is no end to my ability to keep learning. I hope that my pleasure in continuous learning, extended thinking, and self-improvement has been evident in all aspects of this book. I wanted to reveal reflection, deep thought, and conscious presence to be a way of action in my daily life. Self-examination and empowerment have become essential in my everyday life. Nothing I do is impossible; everything I do requires consistency and hard work.

Progressive development has never been a term I didn't understand, but my new definition of consciousness is the root of my lifestyle. I'm forever a work in progress, and I'll continue to appreciate my many stages of enlightenment. Fear and ignorance will not stand in the way of my heightened power as a spiritual being. The absence of these things makes greatness inevitable.

The message I hope was clear: you have the power to live a conscious life, so start at this moment! We all have something to offer to the surrounding universe, be willing to share your energy. Stop waiting for permission to be great, give yourself access to the real power of your soul. We are never powerless when we're drawing from the soul of infinite potential. Our perspective demands a shift to realize this power, now more than ever. My only wish is that this content sparks some thought in our lives to enable us to start a flow of thinking past our unawareness. If we use our internal power to shift our perspective, we are serving the universe:

- Be the remedy for the world.
- Be aware and mindful of your unconsciousness.
- Be open to all soul responses not to empower unconsciousness.

I strive to inspire and serve the universe. My goal is to be me and to uplift those who need inspiration and support through their pure self-will. I want this message to be timeless and applicable for decades.

My favorite quote of all time is by Henry D. Thoreau: "Go confidently in the direction of your dreams! Live the life you've imagined." At every stage of my life, I had a vision of what I wanted my life to be, and I worked towards every goal to achieve that vision. There were never moments of doubt or uncertainty as I didn't prescribe to those feelings. This unforeseen yet expected journey has allowed me to see the vision of my life with a heightened awareness of my real power. I never anticipated peace of mind full of bliss, tranquility, and eternal happiness. This stage is central to my evolution, and I know, through my spiritual principles, that this path design is for me. I'm appreciative of past moments, optimistic about future moments, and beyond grateful for this moment.

I appreciate you and all that you are! I challenge you to be your authentic self, separate from your unconscious mind. Please allow my unconditional love for you to protect you from any difficult situation. Love is the root of happiness, joy, and peace—manifest self-love in your life. Please understanding love and compassion for yourself and others is the only way!

Ascend yourself—your authentic self to higher consciousness.

ABOUT THE AUTHOR

Isaiah A. Tisdale is the author of *His Conscious Perception of the Soul*. He is caring, resilient, ambitious, emotionally intelligent, nurturing, and creative. He was born in Baltimore, MD and grew up in Philadelphia, PA. He holds a B.Sc. from Penn State University in Risk Management and an M.Sc. from Temple University in Finance. Isaiah works across various industries in the financial service sector. Isaiah is the Founder & Owner of tbudget, LLC.

Isaiah became an agent of change in his life before writing his first book. In 2018, the major shift in perspective occurred after his 25th birthday. While he had life-long realizations, soon after his age milestone, the power to be intentional manifested. In 2019, on his journey, Isaiah exercised deliberate strength to become a greater manifestation of his spiritual self. In 2020, he published his first book, *His Conscious Perception of the Soul*. Isaiah resides in Philadelphia, using his creative mind to show his authentic self to the universe.

facebook.com/isaiahatisdale
instagram.com/isaiahatisdale

Made in the USA
Middletown, DE
05 April 2020

88175765R00077